PUB W

IN

Cheshire

THIRTY CIRCULAR WALKS
AROUND CHESHIRE INNS

James F. Edwards

COUNTRYSIDE BOOKS
NEWBURY, BERKSHIRE

First Published 1994
© James F. Edwards 1994
Reprinted 1996

COUNTRYSIDE BOOKS
3 Catherine Road
Newbury, Berkshire

ISBN 1 85306 280 4

*This book is dedicated
to the former members of
Eccles Eighteen Plus Group
whose activities during the
late 60s and early 70s usually
focused upon a pub!*

Designed by Mon Mohan
Cover illustration by Colin Doggett
Photographs and maps by the author

Produced through MRM Associates Ltd., Reading
Typeset by Paragon Typesetters, Queensferry, Clwyd
Printed in England

Contents

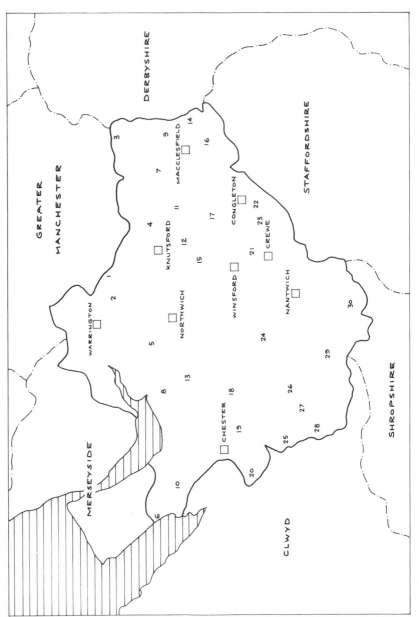

Area map showing locations of the walks.

Publisher's Note

We hope that you obtain considerable enjoyment from this book; great care has been taken in its preparation. However, changes of landlord and actual closures are sadly not uncommon. Likewise, although at the time of publication all routes followed public rights of way or permitted paths, diversion orders can be made and permissions withdrawn.

We cannot of course be held responsible for such diversion orders and any inaccuracies in the text which result from these or any other changes to the routes, nor any damage which might result from walkers trespassing on private property. However, we are anxious that all details covering the walks and the pubs are kept up to date and would therefore welcome information from readers which would be relevant to future editions.

Introduction

Having now completed three walking guides relating to the county of Cheshire, I am still surprised by the diversity of scenery contained within such a small geographical area. However, no amount of descriptive prose can act as a substitute, or adequately compensate, for actually observing this scenery at first-hand. Thus this guide has been written, not to provide light reading, but to be used out in the field to escort the user along the footpaths, highways and byways of rural Cheshire.

The walks have been designed to give a taste of the variety of the Cheshire countryside, whilst at the same time enabling the participants to enjoy the atmosphere and offerings of some of the finest inns in the county.

Partake in a seaside walk on the Wirral Peninsula; meander amongst the hills of the Peak District National Park; walk beside river, mere and canal; stroll across the rich farming country of the central Cheshire Plain and gaze upon characterful black and white dwellings; all this, and a host of idyllic picturesque villages and centuries-old churches just waiting to be explored.

As well as varied scenery, Cheshire can also boast a tremendous variety of inns, making the task of selection a difficult one. The inns at the centre of each walk all have their own innate character and range from the unpretentious but warm, welcoming houses in the hills, to the more sophisticated hostelries found in the villages of the Cheshire Plain.

For centuries the inn has been an intrinsic part of Cheshire life with many of the older establishments having started out as farms which gradually developed into licensed premises. The landlords of these forerunners of present-day Cheshire inns would be amazed at the range of drink and food taken for granted by the modern traveller.

It should be noted that specific opening times have not been included in the individual pub descriptions – due to the fact that they are constantly changing. However, these can always be obtained by using the telephone number which is given at the end of each description. Also, where the menu is the subject of constant change, only an outline of the type of food available is given. Again, each individual pub can be contacted in order to obtain specific menu details.

Furthermore, it must be stressed that parking is only for patrons. Alternative parking locations, when available, have been indicated in the text.

Footwear is important. Waterproof walking shoes or boots are recommended, preferably worn over woollen socks. Smooth-soled shoes should not be worn as they can cause accidents and make walking hard work, especially after wet weather. Lightweight waterproof clothing should always be carried to combat the variable English weather. A small rucksack can be useful for carrying such items as food, cameras, binoculars and the like, which help to make a walk that much more enjoyable.

A prime objective has been to provide direct, no-nonsense route detail for each walk, coupled with a clear accompanying sketch map. For those requiring more detail, the relevant OS Landranger 1:50 000 map numbers are given.

Do not be afraid to venture out during the winter months, for an excursion on a cold clear day when the frost has hardened the ground underfoot can be most rewarding, especially when coupled with a warming drink and a hearty meal taken in pleasant surroundings. However, if you wish to enjoy the facilities of an inn following the completion of a walk please remember to leave muddy walking boots in your car.

Finally, some words of thanks. During the survey I have been accompanied by my mother and Jackie Ridgway, both of whom have made valued contributions to the finished work. I must also thank all the managers and landlords of the various inns for taking time from their busy schedules in order to answer my myriad questions.

James F. Edwards

Little Bollington
The Swan With Two Nicks

1

A very attractive pub in a beautiful setting, the Swan With Two Nicks is close to the Dunham Massey Estate near the rippling waters of the river Bollin. The pub's name refers to the 'nicking' of a swan's beak – a practice that at one time was carried out to determine ownership.

Built in the early 19th century, the inn's interior exudes olde-worlde charm, with low beams, horse brasses and antiques round every corner. During summertime when all the flowers are in bloom the exterior is awash with colour and during winter there are glowing real fires to take away the chill.

A wide range of ale is available including Marston's Pedigree, Boddingtons, Whitbread Castle Eden Ale and Flowers. Dry Blackthorn cider is also served. The pub has a fine reputation for its food, offering a wide choice at sensible prices every day at lunchtime and in the evening. Bar food is served and an extension has been recently completed to enlarge the restaurant facilities. Apart from a wide selection of traditional food, the pub specialises in seafood, offering many tempting dishes which vary with each season.

When the weather is fine you can enjoy the beer garden, where children and well-behaved dogs are welcome.

Telephone: 0161-926 9570.

How to get there: The A56 road connects Altrincham with Lymm and Warrington. About 3 miles from Altrincham there is a roadside hotel called the Stamford Arms. Drive down Park Lane which commences at the side of the Stamford Arms and after ¼ mile arrive at the Swan With Two Nicks.

Parking: There is a car park at the side and rear of the Swan With Two Nicks, which walkers patronising the inn can use. Alternatively, there is a roadside car park adjoining the B5160 ¼ mile from its intersection with the A56.

Length of the walk: 4 miles. Map: OS Landranger 109 Manchester (GR 729870).

It is fortuitous that so many of our footpaths pass through the parklands of great estates, thus giving the walker a glimpse of an environment which is hundreds of years old. This walk will take you through the lovely estate of Dunham Massey with its magnificent hall, where herds of fallow deer roam freely throughout a glorious parkland setting. The route then cuts across Dunham Forest Golf Course to Dunham Town (actually a village) and along the towpath of the Bridgewater Canal before returning to Little Bollington via field paths, lanes and tracks.

The Walk
On leaving the inn turn left and after 80 metres go over a metal footbridge taking you across the river Bollin. A large building on the left has recently been converted into a number of dwellings. A gap at the side of a facing gate takes you on to a fenced-in gravel path. Across the fields, straight ahead and to the left, can be seen the imposing buildings of Dunham Hall. A straight length of path leads to a ladder-stile giving access to the grounds of Dunham Estate. Walk forward along a macadam drive and pass to the right of the old mill where a water-wheel can be seen through a gap in the mill building. The drive takes you to the front entrance of Dunham Hall, which is open to the general public every day of the week except Thursdays and Fridays 12 noon to 5 pm from April to October inclusive. The National Trust inherited the Dunham Estate on the death of Roger Grey, tenth Earl of Stamford, in 1976.

The way forks immediately on passing the entrance drive to the hall. Take the right fork here and follow a long, straight drive between trees. It is in this area that you are likely to see the fallow deer which roam freely throughout the estate. After a straight ½ mile follow the drive as it turns to the left. A ladder-stile close by a lodge house takes you out of the estate and on to a crossing road. Walk over the road, turn right, and then almost immediately turn left to pass through a gap

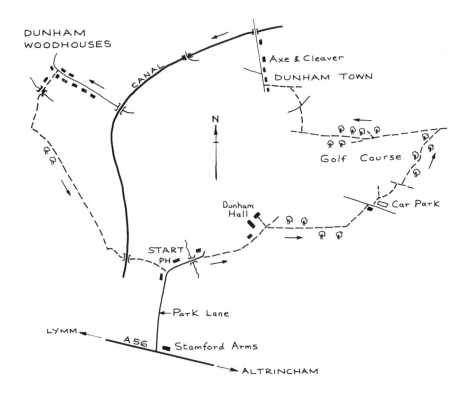

in a wooden fence. On the right is a roadside car park (the alternative starting point for the walk). Keep to the right where the path forks – there is a manhole just before the point where the path forks. The path leads through trees and undergrowth then emerges on to a fairway of the Dunham Forest Golf Club. Walk straight across the fairway – after first checking to ensure that you will not interfere with a golf match – and enter facing trees. The footpath joins a crossing track close to Tee No 12. Turn right along the track then, after only 30 metres, turn left and cross the fairway to follow a well-defined path through trees.

Follow this path until a T-junction is reached at a crossing gravel track. Turn sharp left here and once again walk across the golf course passing close to Tee No 6 (ladies). The track takes you into trees where the track forks; the right fork, by a building, is private, so keep to the left here but, after only a further 20 metres, bear right where the track forks again. A straight section of track leads through quite dense trees. On emerging walk forward and, keeping in the same direction as before, cross two fairways of the golf course then pass to the left of a raised green. On crossing another fairway leave the golf course via a stile in a facing fence. A straight footpath leads along a field edge where there is a hedgerow on the immediate left. At the field corner is a junction of paths. Turn right here where a sign points to Oldfield Lane and follow a field edge with a hedgerow now on your immediate right. At the field corner a stile gives access to Oldfield Lane. Turn right along the lane but, after only 20 metres, turn left to leave the lane over a stile. Cross the next field along a well-worn path and then turn left where a sign points to School Lane. A short section of hedged-in path takes you over a stile and then steps on to School Lane, where the way is to the right.

On the right now is Dunham Town post office and store. Walk past the head of Back Lane and continue. Across the road, on your left, is St Mark's church, built in 1864. Continue past the Axe and Cleaver Inn and the village hall, originally a school built in 1759, to arrive at a bridge which takes you over the Bridgewater Canal. Leave the lane to the right now and descend to the towpath of the canal. Walk under the bridge you have just crossed and continue along the towpath.

Pass under the next bridge and continue along the towpath. After a further ½ mile the canal narrows briefly where a bridge passes over a lane. Leave the towpath to the right just before this bridge and descend along a path to go over a fence-stile close to where a sign indicates 'The Billy Bushell Coppice'. Turn right and follow the pavement along Woodhouse Lane. Shortly pass dwellings and enter the hamlet of Dunham Woodhouses. Just before Yew Tree Farm turn left to enter Meadow Lane, which is a cinder track. Pass cottages and go over the river Bollin via a bridge. Immediately after crossing the bridge leave the track to enter a field and bear diagonally left where a path follows a line of telegraph poles. A footbridge takes you over a tributary of the Bollin. Climb up a facing grassy bank and go over a stile close by a telegraph pole. Walk to the next telegraph pole and turn sharp left – there is a footpath sign here. After 60 metres go over a stile at the side of a field gate. Follow a field edge, keeping a hedgerow on your immediate right. Go over a stile at the field corner to enter a large field. Keep forward now, aiming just to the right of a large electricity pylon which can be seen across the field about 250 metres away. Go over a stile at the side of a field gate close to the pylon. Follow a track and soon pass over another stile at the side of a gate. A facing tunnel takes you under the Bridgewater Canal. The track becomes a cobbled way leading to a junction with a lane.

Turn left now and walk back to the Swan With Two Nicks and the car.

2 Lymm
The Golden Fleece

Lymm is a delightful place with much to interest the inquiring visitor. The village is built on a natural outcrop of sandstone rock out of which the streets have been cut. Part of the rock was utilised during the construction of the villages' best-known landmark, its ancient cross located at the heart of the village.

The Golden Fleece is considered almost as a local for travellers from the nearby canal. It is an attractive, though unusual building, for it has a number of split-level bars. The Village Bar, which is at street level, was once the village cobbler's shop, but is now used as a dining area. Low ceilings, old brassware and fireplaces add to the homely atmosphere. The inn offers a range of Greenalls beers and cask ales, including Original real ale. Draught Strongbow cider is also available. Food is served every lunchtime and in the evening with a selection of roast joints being an additional attraction every Sunday lunchtime. The menu offers a wide choice for every course at very reasonable prices. The starters include soup, oriental parcels, breaded mushrooms and prawn cocktail. The main courses range from the standard steaks, chicken, gammon and mixed grills to chicken tikka masala, beef Sicilian and a variety of seafood dishes. There is also a wide

choice of tempting desserts. Vegetarian dishes are available and the 'Something Different' choices include baby black ribs and turkey char siu. The inn boasts a splendid canal-side beer garden with a separate play area for children.
Telephone: 01925 755538.

How to get there: Lymm is situated between Altrincham and Warrington, with the village centre lying just to the north of the A56. The Golden Fleece is close to the centre of the village near to the bridge which crosses the Bridgewater Canal.

Parking: Walkers patronising the inn are welcome to use the car park at the side and rear. Alternatively, there is a public car park off Pepper Street at the side of Lymm Cross.

Length of the walk: 5 miles. Map: OS Landranger 109 Manchester (GR 683873).

The walk takes in a section of the Bridgewater Canal, crosses agricultural land, passes through the overgrown remains of a once-busy stone quarry, then follows a well-defined bridle-path leading back to the village.

The Walk
From the inn go across the adjacent bridge taking you over the canal. Turn right and follow the canal towpath away from the bridge. Pass close to new property. On the opposite side of the canal is the mooring basin of Lymm Cruising Club. After ¾ mile, pass under Lloyd Bridge and continue along the towpath.

About 1770 the Bridgewater Canal was extended from Worlsey to Runcorn, cutting through the village of Lymm. The canal brought benefits in the form of quicker and cheaper transport, thus boosting local industries. Pass under the next bridge (Grantham's Bridge). About 250 metres further on the canal passes over a lane. Shortly, on the other side of the canal, there are some old mill buildings followed by an array of various workshops and other premises. Continue, and, just before the next bridge (Agden Bridge), leave the towpath to the left, where a kissing-gate gives access to the lane which passes over the bridge. Cross Agden Bridge and turn right. Pass the head of Agden Lane and then the Old Boat House Inn (now a private dwelling) to continue along Warrington Lane. About 300 metres later leave the lane to the left, where a footpath sign points across the fields at 90° to Warrington Lane. After a straight 150 metres, turn right, and continue (you are now walking parallel to Warrington Lane). Your aiming point is between two telegraph poles which can be seen about 150 metres

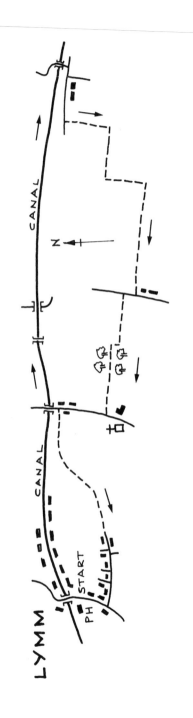

away straight ahead. Arrive at a crossing hedgerow in which the previously mentioned telegraph poles are set. Turn left now and follow the field edge keeping the hedgerow on your immediate right for 200 metres until you arrive at the field corner. Turn right at a facing hedgerow and continue, keeping the hedgerow on your immediate left. At the field corner go over a stile and continue, still keeping a hedgerow on your immediate left. Cross three fields and go over three more stiles to enter a lane where the way is right. After only 30 metres, leave the lane to the left over a stile where there is a footpath sign. Keeping a hedgerow on your immediate left walk towards some trees. Turning right, then left enter the trees over a stile. Follow a path through these trees keeping to the level higher ground. The voids on either side of the path were formed by quarrying the underlying stone used for many local dwellings.

Emerge from the trees over a stile and continue along the edge of a large field, keeping a fence on your immediate left. A church now comes into view straight ahead. A stile gives access to a lane, where the way is right. Descend along the laneside pavement leading to a bridge over the canal. Do not cross the bridge but enter a bridle-path on the left where a sign tells you that Lymm is 1 ½ km distant. After ½ mile, the path emerges at a facing road. Keep forward and pass Ravenbank County Primary School. The facing road leads into the centre of Lymm, close by the ancient cross.

Before turning right and returning to the Golden Fleece and the car spare a few minutes to stroll around a typical Cheshire village.

Disley and Marple
The Romper Inn

The Peak Forest Canal, which connects the Ashton Canal at Dukinfield with Whaley Bridge, was constructed during the final decade of the 18th century – primarily for the transportation of limestone from the Buxton area of Derbyshire. Prior to this time, the site of the Romper Inn was occupied by a row of cottages. The thirsty work of canal building was recognised by the enterprising owners of these cottages with the result that the Romper Inn came into being. The olde-worlde atmosphere of the original building has been retained in the hostelry we see today, and it is well known for its range of beers, where thirst-quenchers such as Wadworth 6X and Theakston Old Peculier compete with the likes of Timothy Taylor Landlord and draught Dry Blackthorn cider.

The inn also has an excellent reputation for its food, which is served every lunchtime and evening (on Sunday, food is served from 12 noon until 9.45 pm). The menu must be one of the most comprehensive of any similar establishment in the north-west. Virtually any type of meal can be purchased and the choice is constantly changing. Keep an eye open for the 'Specials Board' where additional delicacies are chalked up. The inn has a beer garden where children are welcome but the landlord asks that dogs are not taken into the building.

Telephone: 0161-427 1354.

How to get there: The Romper Inn is situated in a somewhat remote place. There are two approaches – one from Marple and the other from High Lane.

From Marple, drive along Church Lane – which commences at the junction of the A626 and A627 roads. Church Lane climbs and becomes Ridge Road which takes you over a hill and on to the Romper Inn.

From High Lane, drive up Carr Brow – which joins the A6 road at a bend on the Disley side – and then turn left to enter Wybersley Road. One mile further along this twisty road brings you to the Romper Inn.

Parking: Ths inn has ample parking for patrons. Alternatively, other parking is available at a car park a little further up the hill from the inn at Ridge Quarry Viewpoint.

Length of the walk: 3 miles. Map: OS Landranger 109 Manchester (GR 965866).

Prior to the boundary changes of 1976, the whole of the walk would have been within the county of Cheshire. Now only half of the route is in this county – the other half being in Greater Manchester. Although this means that the Romper Inn now lies a few hundred yards outside the Cheshire boundary, it has been included because apart from being a fine hostelry, it is the ideal base for an excellent and varied walk. Fortunately, the scenery is just the same as it always was and the walk provides a platform for long views across to the hills of the High Peak. The return leg takes in a section of the Peak Forest Canal prior to climbing back to the Romper Inn along a narrow lane.

The Walk

On leaving the inn descend along a laneside footpath, then keep left into Turf Lea. After 50 metres, turn right and pass over a stone stile to enter a field. A straight path takes you to a stile which is located about 20 metres to the right of a row of houses. On passing over this stile follow a field edge, pass over another stile, then skirt around a small pond. After the next stile the path is fenced in. Shortly, there is a junction of paths. Keep forward here in the direction of Jackson's Edge. Walk across the corner of a field, then go over a stile in a crossing fence. There is an isolated stone chimney about 50 metres away on the left here. A broad, grassy path climbs to a facing gate which you go through and ascend along a stony track through trees. Emerge from the trees and cross one of the fairways of Disley Golf Course. Keep to the left of a facing bank to follow a track which gradually climbs. On the right you will see a short, squat circular

17

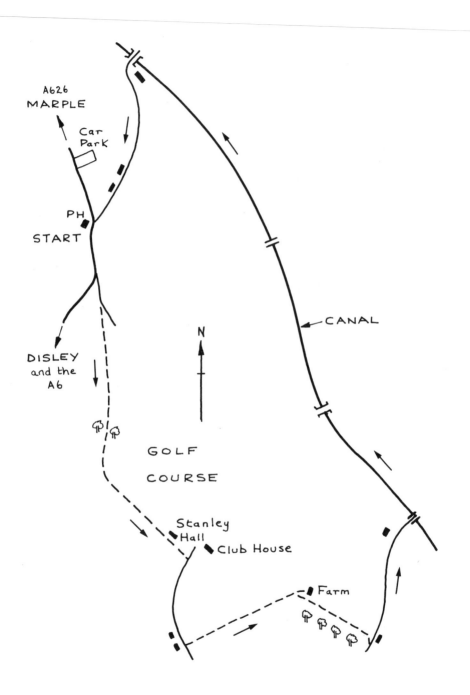

air-vent leading from a railway tunnel which passes under the golf course. The track turns to the left and continues across the golf course where there are long views to the distant hills of the Peak National Park.

After you pass Stanley Hall there is a junction of ways. Down to the left is the large club house belonging to the golf course, but turn right here to gradually ascend along a macadam drive. On the left shortly is an interesting wooden shelter topped by a weather-vane. As you emerge from Disley Golf Course turn left and go over a stile at the side of a field gate where a sign points to Higgins Clough. Follow a track which gradually descends across a field. There is another air-vent from the railway tunnel shortly on the left. The track leads to a gate which gives access to a farm, but turn right and leave the track about 20 metres before the gate to pass through a gap in a hedge. Descend across a narrow field keeping the farm outbuildings about 30 metres away to your left. Go over a stile in a crossing fence and descend along the right-hand edge of a large sloping field. There are long views to the facing hills from this section of the path. Cross a stile to emerge on to a narrow lane close to a dwelling. Turn left and ascend the lane past the entrance drive of Haycroft, then descend to go over a counterbalanced bridge giving access to the towpath of the Peak Forest Canal. Turn left and walk beside the canal, an endless source of fascination with its boats and wildlife.

Down on the right is the valley of the river Goyt where gaps through the trees offer glimpses of the village of Strines.

Follow the towpath for 1 mile, passing under bridges 23 and 21 en route. After bridge 21 leave the towpath and walk over the bridge. Bear left and follow a narrow lane past the rear of a couple of dwellings fronting the canal; one of these is called Clough Bridge Cottage. The lane climbs past a number of dwellings and takes you back to the Romper Inn and the car.

Mobberley
The Bull's Head and Roebuck Inns

Mobberley can boast of a long history, going back centuries before its mention in the Domesday Book. The village possesses many attractive and interesting buildings of varied styles which are a delight to the discerning visitor.

Mobberley can also boast two superb inns, both dating back to the 17th century and only metres apart at the start of a splendid walk! It would have been unfair to leave one out, therefore both have been included.

The Bull's Head has open coal fires, a wealth of oak beams, its own bowling green and a beer garden. Inside, the walls are adorned with photographs of old Mobberley. The inn provides traditional hand-pulled ales from Tetley, Boddingtons and Jennings of Cumbria. Draught Strongbow cider is also available. There is a range of real home-cooked lunches at very reasonable prices. Home-made pies vie with authentic Indian curries and the desserts include hot chocolate fudge cake and apple and blackberry pancake rolls. For snacks you can choose from a wide range of traditional and toasted sandwiches.

During recent years the Roebuck was internally modernised using floorboards recycled from a local mill and the seating is in the form of pews. There is an adjacent beer garden. The inn serves beers from Boddingtons, Ruddles, Courage and John Smith's together with Scrumpy and draught Strongbow cider. Food is available every lunchtime and evening. Two menus are always provided, one for full meals and the other for snacks. The choice includes several daily special dishes. The range of food is excellent and varies with the season, each main course being complemented by locally grown produce.

Telephone: 01565 873134 (Bull's Head).
Telephone: 01565 872757 (Roebuck).

How to get there: Mobberley straddles the B5085 between Knutsford and Wilmslow. The road dips through a hollow on the Wilmslow side of the village at the junction with Mill Lane. Drive along Mill Lane and after 150 metres arrive at the inns.

Parking: Both inns have car parks. Alternatively, park on Mill Lane, although space is somewhat limited.

Length of the walk: 3 ½ miles. Map: OS Landranger 118 Stoke-on-Trent and Macclesfield (GR 789796).

The walk heads away from the village along lanes, tracks and cross-country paths then through the parish of Great Warford before returning along a delightful path which never strays too far away from the bubbling waters of Mobberley Brook.

The Walk

Enter a narrow lane which commences opposite the Bull's Head and runs along one side of the Roebuck car park. Climb along the lane past Damson Cottage where it becomes a grassy track. After 300 metres the track turns sharply to the right at a facing gate and stile. Turn right and follow the track as it gradually climbs between hedges. Go through a wooden gate and continue. The track peters out shortly and becomes a path which takes you along a field edge. There are long views from this section of path over to the left now, where the hill at Alderley Edge is visible.

Follow the path as it turns to the left at the field corner. After a further 80 metres arrive at a field gate on the right from where a modern barn is visible across the fields about 400 metres away. Go through the gate and walk along the edge of a large rough field with a hedgrow on your immediate right. Turn left at the field corner and continue, still with a hedgerow on your right. Pass between the modern barn and the hedgerow on your right to arrive at a gate which gives access to a macadam drive. Turn left and walk along the drive.

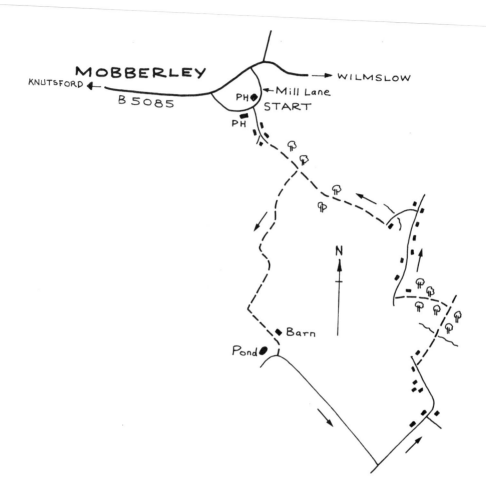

A straight ½ mile leads to a crossing lane, where the way is left. You are now walking along Pedley House Lane. A straight ¼ mile takes you past a lane which goes off to the right. Enter Faulkner's Lane and follow this as it bends to the left. Pass a development of new homes and a little further on leave the lane to the right, where a stile at the side of a gate gives access to a field. This path begins opposite a renovated black and white dwelling where a footpath sign points across the field. Follow the field edge keeping a hedgerow on your immediate left. At the field corner go over a footbridge and stile which takes you across Mobberley Brook. There is a fence on the left side of the path now. About 150 metres after crossing the brook go over a stile on the left, where there is a footpath sign. Keep to the right of trees then, after a further 60 metres, enter facing trees via a plank-bridge and stile. Climb forward up a grassy bank. Straight ahead there is a dwelling. Walk forward and keep to the left of the garden hedge to arrive at a stile at the side of a gate. Cross the stile to once again enter Faulkner's Lane, where the way is right. Gradually climb and pass the ornate entrance gate of Antrobus Hall.

After a further 250 metres turn left to enter a macadam drive commencing at the side of a house called Merrydale. There is a footpath sign here and a board indicating Coppuck House. Follow the drive over Mobberley Brook, pass Coppuck House, go through a facing gate and then turn right to pass over a stile which is at the side of a gate. Follow a field edge, keeping a hedgerow on your immediate right. At the field corner go through a gate and continue, again with a hedgerow on your immediate right. At the next field corner, which is sometimes boggy, go over a stile and climb up a bank to enter a large undulating field. Cross the field, bearing slightly right, to arrive at a stile by a facing gate. Cross the stile and walk forward along a track.

You are now back on part of the route you took earlier in the walk. The track leads back to the lane which in turn takes you back to the inn and the car.

Lower Whitley
The Chetwode Arms

5

Named after a family of local landowners, much of the building which is today the Chetwode Arms is over 300 years old. The inn is very near St Luke's church and this closeness was used to good effect when the old custom of 'roping' used to take place. After a wedding, the route of the happy couple was barred by a rope which was only removed on payment of the price of a good drink. This custom was carried out as recently as 1968.

The inn has many rooms and two bars. The lounge, with its sloping floor, has french windows opening on to an attractive bowling green. Greenall Whitley beers are served including mild, bitter and hand-pulled original ale as well as draught Strongbow cider. The Chetwode Arms is well known for its fine food, served at lunchtime and in the evening. A traditional menu is supplemented by a large specials board resulting in an extremely wide choice. There is a beer garden, and a play area for children adjoins the car park. If the weather is fine refreshments may be taken at tables overlooking the immaculate bowling green. In cooler weather there are no less than five real fires to warm you.

Telephone: 01925 730203.

How to get there: Lower Whitley is just off the A49 6 miles to the south of Warrington and 2 miles to the south of junction 10 of the M56. The Chetwode Arms is at the centre of the village not far from the church.

Parking: The inn has a large car park. Alternatively, there is a parking lay-by at the side of the A49 about 300 metres from Street Lane, which leads into the village of Lower Whitley.

Length of the walk: 3 ½ miles. Map: OS Landranger 118 Stoke-on-Trent and Macclesfield (GR 614789).

There are two Whitleys, once variously known as Over and Nether Whitley, Whitley Superior and Inferior; now the names have settled into Higher and Lower Whitley. Today's jaunt provides an opportunity to explore both places. The first half of the walk is along field paths and over stiles followed by a gentle mile along a narrow, half-forgotten, rural lane on the approaches to Higher Whitley. A short stroll around the village precedes the return to Lower Whitley along a lane taking you between half-hidden pools where fishermen from near and far practice their skills.

The Walk

Enter a hedged-in footpath directly opposite the inn. Pass to the rear of the church grounds and leave the path over a stile. Keep forward, in the same direction as before, and pass close to the corner of a fence to a stile. Cut across the corner of a field and after 70 metres go over a stile at the side of a telegraph pole. Follow the edge of a large field, keeping a hedgerow on your immediate left. Go through a gate at the field corner and bear right to follow a farm approach track. after 60 metres go through a facing gate and turn left just before the farmyard to go over a stile at the side of another gate. Keep close by the farm garden hedgerow and follow it to the right after about 20 metres. A straight 80 metres leads to a stile in a crossing-fence. Go over the stile, then bear left to pass close to a fenced-in pond half overgrown with bullrushes. On passing the pond bear left to go over a stile in a facing fence to the left of a small copse. Continue, keeping a fence on your immediate right, to walk along the edge of a large field. About 30 metres before the field corner is reached go over a stile in the fence on your right and continue in the same direction as before with the fence, and then a hedgerow, on your left.

As you approach a large wood go over a stile at the field corner and then turn left along a field edge with the wood on your right. There is a pond among the trees on your right. The path meanders around the edge of the wood. Where the trees finish there are two square brick and concrete manhole structures about 2 metres square. From this point the way is along a track which gradually climbs towards

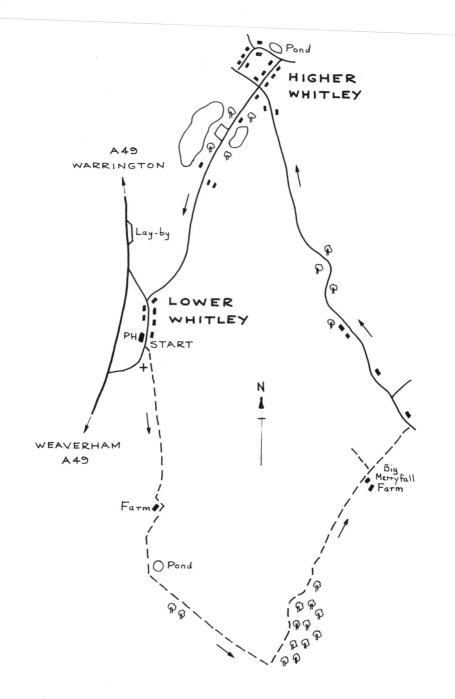

Pond

HIGHER
WHITLEY

A49
WARRINGTON

Lay-by

LOWER
WHITLEY

PH START

WEAVERHAM
A49

N

Big
Merryfall
Farm

Farm

Pond

buildings. The track follows a field edge where there is a hedgerow on the left. The track takes you to the left of Big Merryfall Farm. Pass a track going off to the left and follow a straight stretch of track taking you to a crossing lane. Turn left along the lane which shortly turns sharply to the right, but keep forward here to enter Back Lane. On passing a three-storey dwelling, built in 1741, the lane becomes a hedged-in track. Emerge at a facing gate and follow the track along a field edge. Pass through another gate and continue past a couple of dwellings on the left. The track has given way to a narrow winding macadam lane taking you to a crossroads on the edge of the village of Higher Whitley.

The route back to Lower Whitley is along Village Lane off to the left, but first turn to the right and take a look at the village of Higher Whitley.

The village has retained an old-fashioned atmosphere and has many interesting buildings. On the next left turning there is a delightful scene across a large pond which is the home of many species of water fowl. Turn next left and pass the head of Dark Lane. On turning left again you will arrive back at the crossroads opposite Back Lane.

Turn right now to proceed along Village Lane. Pass the school and shortly arrive at a walled-in burial area on the right. This is a Quaker burial ground where the oldest recorded burial relates to John Starkey (1657). During the religious conflicts of the 17th century, Quakers (the Society of Friends) were a persecuted sect not permitted the rites of the established church. Consequently members had to be buried in remote spots such as this. At the rear of the burial ground you will see the deep waters of Whitley Pool. Village Lane leads to the outskirts of Lower Whitley where the way is left to pass Village Farm. A few more strides and you are back at the Chetwode Arms.

6 **Parkgate**
The Red Lion Inn

Parkgate was a bustling port during the 18th and early 19th centuries, with ships regularly sailing to Ireland. Today, it is hard to imagine deep water lapping against the sea wall, although an occasional high tide gives some impression of how things must have appeared then. When the roads to Holyhead were improved the journey by sea to Ireland was halved, and the fortunes of Parkgate declined. The ensuing silting of the Dee Estuary ended the villages' role as a port.

Before the estuary silted up, the Red Lion Inn was only a few yards away from the sea. The building dates from about 1710 and subsequent records show that it was used as a trading house during the early part of the 19th century. Outside there hangs an ornate and rare Walker's sign, whilst the interior of the inn exudes character with all sorts of brick-à-brac lining the low ceilings and the walls. The beams are authentic, and high-backed seats create a cosy traditional atmosphere.

This is a Peter Walker house, with a good choice of ales including Walker Best Bitter and Dark Mild and Ind Coope Burton Ale. Olde English draught cider is also available. Meals are served every day between 12 noon and 2 pm. There is usually a choice of soups and the main courses vary with the seasons. Fresh fish is featured on the menu, together with such dishes as steak and kidney, chilli and rice, liver and onions, and Cumberland sausages. Snacks include baked potatoes with a choice of fillings, and toasted sandwiches. Vegetarians are also catered for. There is a small selection of sweets from which to choose. Telephone: 0151-336 1548.

How to get there: The A540 connects Chester with Hoylake on the Wirral peninsula. Approximately midway the secondary B5134 runs in a westerly direction from the A540 and, after 1 mile, passes through Neston; then it is a further mile to Parkgate. The Red Lion Inn fronts on to The Parade, a long promenade, looking out across the Dee Estuary.

Parking: Although the inn does not have its own car park, parking is allowed on certain sections of The Parade (check signs for details). Alternatively, there is a public car park off School Lane, which joins The Parade 200 metres from the inn.

Length of the walk: 4½ miles. Map: OS Landranger 117 Chester and 108 Liverpool (GR 279782).

This is a Cheshire walk with a difference for it has a distinct seaside flavour. The old port of Parkgate is a delightful place with many characterful houses and fishermen's cottages. The long promenade has old-fashioned shops selling fresh seafood and home-made ice-cream. The walk, which is flat and easy going, takes you along the promenade and then out to the north of the town where a footpath follows the sea wall. The route then cuts inland along a lane to join the Wirral Way for the return journey to Parkgate.

The Walk
Turn right on leaving the inn and walk along The Parade. The wide expanse of the Dee Estuary on your left-hand side reaches across to the shores of Wales and, if the day is clear you should be able to make out the dark shape of Flint Castle 7 miles away.

On reaching the end of The Parade, the road turns to the right and becomes Boathouse Lane, but keep forward here to pass in front of the Boat House Inn. A sign further on indicates Wirral Country Park. The way leads to a parking area for vehicles at the end of which there is a junction of footpaths. A sign to the right points towards the Wirral Way, but keep forward here to cross a facing stile. Follow a path which hugs the shoreline and follows the course of the sea wall.

This area is a favourite location for bird-watchers who come with their binoculars and telescopes to observe the various species.

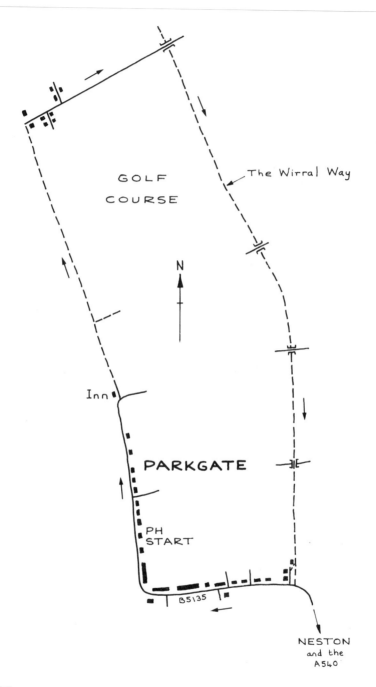

GOLF
COURSE

The Wirral Way

N

Inn

PARKGATE

PH
START

B5135

NESTON
and the
A540

Shortly, over to the right, there is a golf course and a little further on the footpath actually runs along the top of the sea wall. The path takes you, via steps, to a lane at the side of Gayton Cottage, which has a rather unusual clock set in a miniature ornate tower above its garage. Follow the lane and pass Cottage Drive West. The lane gradually climbs now to tall hedgerows on both sides then passes over a bridge. Leave the lane to the right after a further 50 metres, through a gap by a gate where a sign indicates Wirral Country Park. Descend to a footpath created from the defunct Neston to Hoylake railway line. Turn left, and walk away from the bridge you have just crossed; that is, in the direction of Neston. Follow a clearly defined tree-lined path that cuts across the golf course you glimpsed earlier in the walk.

You are walking along the Wirral Way, part of a linear park which has been created for the enjoyment of walkers in the Wirral. There are a number of strategically positioned seats along the way where you can rest and enjoy the views across the Dee Estuary.

Almost 1 mile after joining the Wirral Way, pass under Backwood Hall Bridge and continue along the footpath. After a further 500 metres, pass under Boathouse Lane Bridge and continue along the Wirral Way. A little over ¼ mile further on, pass over a bridge which takes the footpath over a lane. The path is elevated in this area and quite heavily wooded on both sides and takes you to facing undergrowth. Turn right and then left to follow a cobbled way which in the days of the railway, was an approach to Parkgate Station. Emerge on to Rope Walk, turn left, and after 30 metres arrive at a crossing-road. Turn right and walk along the roadside pavement past Grenfell Park.

Shortly on the right, and opposite the Old Quay Hotel, there is a row of cottages. The end cottage (No 16) is said to be the place where the then Emily Lyon stayed in June 1784 when she came to Parkgate to take the waters in an attempt to cure a skin complaint. Later she became Lady Emma Hamilton and subsequently the mistress of Lord Nelson.

Turn right on passing the cottages and walk along The Parade. The large black and white building on the right is Mostyn House School. During the 18th century this building was an inn and records tell us that the great German composer George Frederick Handel stayed here. The noted medical missionary, Sir Wilfred Thomason Grenfell, was born at Mostyn House in 1865. He went on to establish hospitals, missions and homes in Labrador and Newfoundland and was knighted in 1927.

A little further along The Parade is one of Parkgate's well-known home-made ice-cream shops, and if you wish you can enjoy this refreshment as you walk back to the car.

7 Mottram St Andrew
The Bull's Head Inn

Diagonally across the road from the Bull's Head Inn is Mottram Cross, an old butter cross, having a 14th century base and a restored shaft and head dated 1832. The coat of arms on the cross is that of the Wright family of Mottram, whose crest, depicting a bulls head over a crown, is that shown on the colourful signboard of the inn.

This very attractive inn is over 400 years old and was previously a farm with a six day licence to sell liquor. Although the inn has a large interior there are many quiet corners in which to relax. Owned by Whitbread, the beer on offer includes Castle Eden Ale, a rich sweetish bitter. Boddingtons beers are also served, and draught Strongbow cider. An extensive choice of food is available ranging from soup, freshly filled sandwiches, ploughman's lunch, stuffed jacket potatoes, steak 'n' kidney pie, lasagne, Cumberland sausages, fisherman's pie and chicken combo to chocolate fudge cake and apple pie, all of which can be purchased as bar food. Also, a range of meals with all the trimmings is served in a separate restaurant. Food is available at lunchtime and during the evening Monday to Saturday and on Sunday between 12 noon and 10 pm.

The inn has a beer garden and a play area for children.

Telephone: 01625 828694.

How to get there: The A538 connects Wilmslow with Prestbury. The Bull's Head Inn fronts on to this road 2 miles from Prestbury.

Parking: There is a large car park to both sides of the Bull's Head Inn.

Length of the walk: 4 miles. Map: OS Landranger 118 Stoke-on-Trent and Macclesfield (GR 881785).

If you enjoy variety then you will certainly appreciate this walk along lanes, paths, tracks, climbs and descents, streams and woods, and above all the magnificent views across the rolling plains of Cheshire and beyond. The initial stages of the walk take you to the slopes of Daniel Hill and then close to the hill at Alderley Edge prior to crossing a plateau which skirts the parkland setting of Hare Hill Estate. The return leg of the journey is along tracks, lanes and field paths.

The Walk
On leaving the inn, turn left and enter Priest Lane. Gradually descend past Brook House Farm, Brook Cottage and Mottram House. Leave the lane to the left now, before it starts to ascend, and enter a hedged-in track over a stile at the side of a gate, where a footpath sign points away from the road. After 80 metres there is a junction of paths. Turn right here where a footpath sign points towards Oak Road. Gradually climb along a grassy track. The way continues between widely spaced hedges. Emerge from the hedged-in way at a stile and enter a field. Walk forward along the field edge, keeping a hedgerow on your immediate left and shortly pass a low-set pond. The hedgerow turns to the left but keep forward here to the facing field corner to go over a stile giving access to a lane at the right-hand side of a house. Turn right and then, after 40 metres, leave the lane over a stile on the left where a footpath sign points away from the lane. Follow a field edge, keeping a hedgerow on your immediate right. After 60 metres go over a stile in a crossing-fence and continue, still with a hedge on your immediate right.

Over to the right you will see a large pond which is a favourite haunt of local fishermen. A stile at the field corner gives access to a wood. Descend along a steep section of path now, cross a stream via a plank, then ascend to emerge from the wood over a stile. Continue along the edge of a field, keeping a hedgerow on your immediate left. The hill at Alderley Edge is visible straight ahead. At the field corner go over a stile and continue across the next field where a well-defined path takes you to the right of a dwelling. Cross the entrance drive to the dwelling and immediately go over a stile in a facing hedgerow to enter a large, sloping field. Bear left now and climb past the dwelling, keeping a hedgerow on your left. A facing stile leads into a wood, but

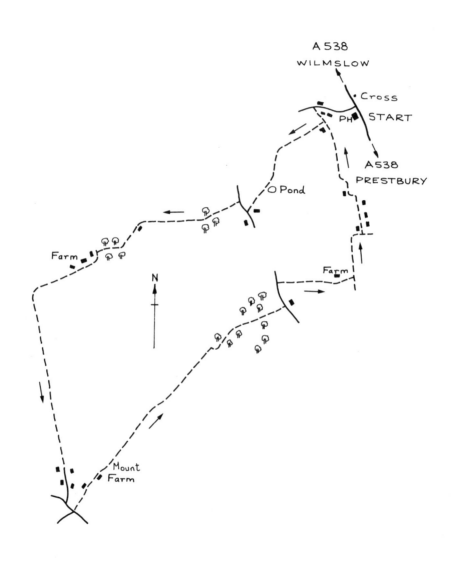

before negotiating this, look back at long views towards Stockport and beyond. On crossing the stile turn right and ascend along a path which keeps near the edge of the wood. There is a junction of paths at the top of the climb where outbuildings can be seen straight ahead. To the left there is a concessionary path to Hare Hill Estate but the way is right here to ascend steps and over a slab-stile. Straight ahead can be seen a flight of steps and a sign indicating The Edge – but ignore this and turn left to go through a gateway close to the outbuildings. After 25 metres turn right before a facing gate is reached and walk along a concrete drive which takes you to the left of a farm. Follow the drive away from the farm, pass a small bungalow, then go over a stile at the side of a cattle grid. The drive turns to the left. Keep along the drive. After almost ½ mile, the drive emerges on to a facing macadam lane. The lane takes you to a crossing road where the way is left. After 25 metres turn left again to follow a rough track towards Mount Farm where a footpath sign points away from the road.

Pass a dwelling on your left and then pass close to the farmhouse where a gate gives access to a hedged-in track leading away from the farm. After ¼ mile the track is no longer hedged in. The track takes you close to trees on the right. Keep an eye open for a stile which gives access to the trees where a sign indicates Hare Hill. Cross this stile and follow a well-maintained path through trees where there is a stream on your right. Emerge from the trees and go through a small metal gate. There is a concessionary path which goes directly off to Hare Hill on the right here, but this is not the path to take. With the metal gate at your back walk forward and gently ascend to the right of facing trees to enter a large undulating field surrounded by trees. Cross the first undulation in the field bearing diagonally to your right and then gradually descend to pass throuh a gap at the field edge. (This gap is about 160 metres from the small metal gate which you passed through previously.) Climb diagonally right now, to follow a well-worn footpath across a field in the direction of a dwelling you will see straight ahead. Go through a gate and emerge onto a lane in front of the dwelling. Turn left along the lane.

After 120 metres, leave the lane to the right over a stile, where a footpath sign points away from the lane. Walk straight across the facing field to go over a stile at the side of a gate. Continue along a field edge, keeping a fence on your right. At the field corner pass over another stile and continue with a fence now on the immediate left. At the field corner go over a narrow stile at the side of a gate. Straight ahead are the buildings of Allen's Farm. Bear slightly right, walk forward and descend, then go over a stile at the side of a gate about 25 metres to the right of twin telegraph poles which carry an electrical device. Descend, and bear left. At the bottom of the descent go over a concrete plank taking you over a narrow brook, and then cross a stile to enter a hedged-in track. Turn left and follow the track past the entrance drive of Allen's Farm. The track is level at first and then turns to the right and climbs. After a further 60 metres leave the track to the left where a footpath commences through a narrow gap at the side of a wooden garage. Go up steps and cross a stile. The path follows a hedge on the right and takes you past the gardens of large dwellings. Over to the left you will see the dark, murky waters of Hunter's Pool.

The way becomes hedged in for a short distance and leads to a stile at the side of a gate. There is a small thatched cottage on the left here. Go over the stile and turn left to pass through a wooden gate in front of the cottage and then turn right at a facing hedgerow to cross a stile which takes you into an orchard. Walk forward and gradually descend to go over a stile in a crossing fence. There are outbuildings on the left here and various pens used for rearing poultry, so please take care in this area. Bear left now and cross a stout wooden footbridge over a stream. Cross a stile and follow a path through trees which stays parallel with the stream on your right. Emerge from the trees at a stile. Walk forward to pass close to a dwelling and then go over a stile at the side of a facing gate. Walk straight over a macadam drive to shortly pass over another stile. There is a junction of paths now, bear right here where the sign points towards Priest Lane.

You are now back on part of your original route. The facing track leads to Priest Lane where the way is right for the short climb back to the Bull's Head Inn.

Fivecrosses
The Traveller's Rest

8

An unpretentious roadside inn which was built in 1834, the Traveller's Rest is notable for its lunches and evening meals which are complemented by a range of Greenalls beers and draught Strongbow cider. The inn is very compact and has a separate room for dining and a small adjoining bar.

Meals are served every lunchtime and during the evening and from 12 noon until 10.30 pm each Sunday. Starters include soup of the day, egg mayonnaise, prawn cocktail, garlic mushrooms and Florida cocktail. Main courses comprise prime sirloin steak, half a roast chicken, gammon, scampi, trout, lasagne, chicken Kiev, plaice and home-made steak and mushroom pie. There is a wide choice of desserts and special ice-creams and an extensive range of coffees. Salads, ploughman's lunches and vegetarian dishes are also available. Children are welcome and can choose from their own separate menu if required. Drinks can be taken outside if the weather permits using a number of picnic tables situated on a patio area. There is also a children's play area in the garden.

Telephone: 01928 735125.

How to get there: The B5152 climbs out of Frodsham on its route towards Delamere. The Traveller's Rest fronts on to this road at Fivecrosses, about 1½ miles from Frodsham.

Parking: There is a two-tiered car park at the side of the inn. Alternative, usually limited, roadside parking is available on an area of rough ground opposite the inn.

Length of the walk: 3½ miles. Map: OS Landranger 117 Chester (GR 530763).

The main attraction of this walk is a series of splendid views across the Cheshire Plain. However, because the walk commences at a reasonable elevation, this does not involve any great exertion on the part of the walker, and there are only two very moderate gradients to tackle. The initial stages of the walk utilise a typical narrow Cheshire lane followed by a cross-country path which passes close to the historic site of Peel Hall. A further section of lane is followed by a gentle climb to Newton prior to a leisurely descent back to Fivecrosses.

The Walk

On leaving the inn, go over the road and turn left to follow the roadside pavement. After 150 metres, enter a narrow lane on the right which commences at the side of a farm. After ¼ mile the lane turns sharply to the left. Enter a facing farm approach track here. On passing a small bungalow, The Croft, on the right go over a stile on the right where there is a footpath sign. This stile is about 60 metres before the farm is reached. On crossing the stile you have entered a large field. Walk forward, keeping a fence and hedgerow on your immediate right to follow the field edge. At the field corner go over a stile at the side of a gate and follow a facing track which converges with a hedgerow on the right and takes you along the field edge. The track winds and leads to a stile at the side of a gate. Cross the stile and walk forward to go over a crossing track. Bear left to follow a track which takes you in the general direction of the farm you will see about 300 metres away. Shortly, the track turns sharply to the left and leads to the farm, but go over a stile on the right here to enter a field. Turn left now to follow the course of a wall surrounding the farm precincts. The farm, Peel Hall, is privately owned and dates back to the Elizabethan period. If you look closely you will observe that the building is surrounded by a moat.

Where the wall finishes continue along the field edge but with a hedgerow now on the immediate left. At the field corner go over a stile at the side of a gate where there is a small plantation of conifer trees on the right. Follow a hedged-in path which descends. After

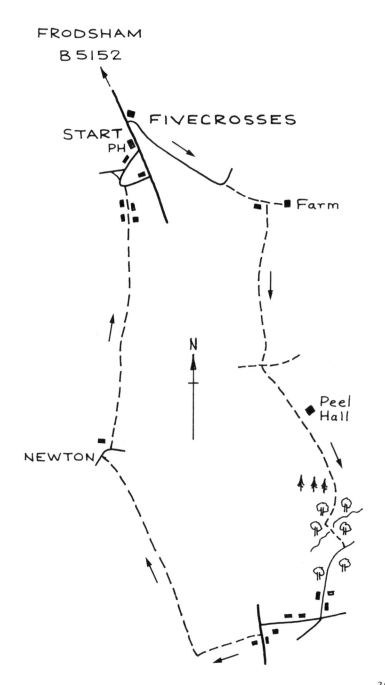

FRODSHAM
B 5152

FIVECROSSES

START
PH

Farm

N

Peel
Hall

NEWTON

39

50 metres turn left to go over a stile at the side of an electricity pole. Follow a narrow hedged-in path for 60 metres and then go over a stile leading to a substantial wooden footbridge. A short climb up an embankment takes you to a stile in a hedgerow. Cross the stile to enter a narrow lane. Turn right along the lane.

After ¼ mile arrive at a junction where a sign informs that you have just walked along Pike Lane. Turn right and follow the roadside pavement in the direction of Frodsham. Pass dwellings and keep on past Mond Primary Science Centre. On reaching a crossing road turn left. After only 20 metres go over the road to cross a stile at the side of a facing gate. Walk forward now along a field edge and gradually climb in the general direction of a pylon visible on higher ground straight ahead. Climb up steps at the field corner and go over a stile in a crossing hedgerow to enter another field. Turn right here and continue, with the hedgerow on your immediate right, to walk along the edge of a large undulating field. Go over a stile in the field corner and cross the next field in the direction of a stile at the side of a gate about 120 metres away. On crossing the stile you have entered a lane. Turn right, but after only 30 metres, leave the lane to the left to follow a path which climbs away from the lane. There is a hedgerow on the immediate right here and a modern detached dwelling on the left. As well as the hedgerow on the right there is now a fence on the left. Go through a facing gate and proceed along more level terrain. Pass through another gate and continue. Shortly, the fence on the left turns away to the left, but keep forward here and go through a facing gate. Continue along a field edge with a hedgerow on your immediate right. At the field corner there is just enough room to squeeze between a gatepost and the hedgerow on the right. Walk forward, in the same direction as before, with the hedgerow on your immediate right. If the day is clear there are extremely long views over the Cheshire Plain from this section of the path.

At the field corner go through a gap in the hedgerow on the right and follow a track, initially along the edge of a rough field, and then between hedges. The track leads past dwellings and emerges at a bend in a crossing-lane. Turn left, and then almost immediately fork right, and then bear right again. The lane descends to the Frodsham road where it emerges at the side of the Traveller's Rest.

9 Rainow
The Robin Hood Inn

The Robin Hood Inn sits above the scattered village of Rainow where the hills and stone buildings are a sharp contrast to the mellow brick and more gentle countryside of the Cheshire Plain. The inn has stood here for many years and was previously known as the Robin Hood and Little John. By 1834 Little John appears to have fallen out of favour for after that date the inn has been recorded simply as the Robin Hood. Exactly where the connection with Robin Hood comes from is unknown. The inn is an unpretentious homely place where draught cider, a range of Greenalls Whitley beers and a good choice of inexpensive meals can be consumed in a warm and friendly atmosphere. Meals are served daily at lunchtime and in the evenings, and a wide range of main courses includes mixed grill, steaks, pies, and house specialities of which an appropriate dish is Friar Tuck Yorkshire Pudding with beef and onion filling.

If the weather happens to be on the chilly side the landlord ensures that his guests have the benefit of roaring log fires in the bar, dining area and family room. There is also an outdoor beer garden where customers may eat their own food when meals are not available, assuming that drinks are bought of course.

Telephone: 01625 574060.

How to get there: Rainow lies on the A5002 3 miles to the north-east of Macclesfield. The Robin Hood Inn fronts on to this road on the north side of the village.

Parking: There is a large car park for patrons at the side of the inn, and alternative limited laneside parking in Smithy Lane, which commences at the side of the inn.

Length of the walk: 3 ½ miles. Map: OS Landranger 118 Stoke-on-Trent and Macclesfield (GR 953762).

There can be no doubt about the main attraction of this walk – the magnificent views over the Cheshire Plain and the hills of the Peak National Park seen from a path which traverses the backbone of Kerridge Hill. The unusual edifice of White Nancy is a place to tarry whilst taking in a view over Bollington where many of the stone buildings remind us of the industries of the 18th and 19th centuries. The area has long been associated with quarrying and the local stone is considered to be of excellent quality; indeed, the cathedral at Coventry is paved with Kerridge stone. The walk returns to Rainow via field paths, tracks and lanes.

The Walk

On leaving the Robin Hood Inn enter Stocks Lane which commences almost opposite the entrance to the car park. This lane takes its name from the location of the village stocks which sit on a bank close to the head of the lane. Follow the lane as it descends past Chapel Lane to join the Macclesfield road. Cross here and follow the roadside pavement descending past the church.

At the bottom cross over the infant river Dean and then climb past the war memorial. The roadside pavement reaches more level terrain. Opposite to the termination of the roadside pavement is the start of a footpath where a sign indicates Kerridge Hill (1 km). This footpath commences at the side of Lane Edge cottage.

Follow a track between stone walls. On emerging from the walled-in track follow a level path which takes you along the edge of a field. Pass over a stile at the end of the field and continue with a stone wall and hawthorn trees on your immediate left. After 100 metres go over a stone stile close by a holly bush. Immediately on crossing this the path forks. There is a level grassy track straight ahead but take a deep breath and climb the left-hand path to the side of Kerridge Hill.

The path leads to a stile in a crossing stone wall. Rest for a minute or two here and admire the view over Rainow and to the hills beyond. Continue up the hillside (the going is easier now) and emerge on the backbone ridge of Kerridge Hill via a stile. Turn right and proceed along a ridge top path which hugs a wall on the right.

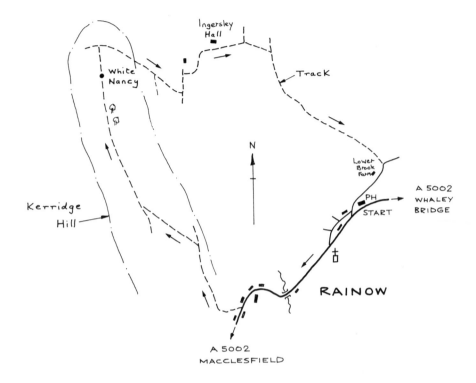

The views from this ridge top path are quite superb. Pass over a couple of stiles and arrive at White Nancy. This edifice resembles a whitewashed sugar loaf and was built in memory of the Battle of Waterloo. Until recently it was possible to sit inside, but because of vandalism the entrance has now been blocked up. White Nancy looks straight out over the town of Bollington where the silver threads of the Macclesfield Canal can be picked out as it winds past dwelling and mill.

From White Nancy descend along a steep path which takes you down the facing hillside. At a crossing drive turn right and pass through a gate at the side of a cattle grid. Keep left shortly to descend along a narrow lane, between walls at first, and then with a wall only on the right. Pass over a cattle grid then turn left at the junction ahead to follow a gravel track. After 50 metres leave the track over a stile on the right which takes you into a field. Shortly pass over a small stone bridge then bear left to climb along a grassy track taking you up the side of a bank. Ascend steps, pass through a stone stile, then enter a large hillside field. Keep along the left side of the field where there is

43

a wall on the immediate left. On the other side of the wall is Ingersley Hall, once the home of the Gaskill family who were responsible for the construction of White Nancy.

Cross two stiles to enter a large field. Ignore a stone stile on the left here and keep forward in the same general direction as before, gradually bearing right to diverge away from a stone wall on your left. A stile made of stone blocks which is set in a gateway gives access to a walled-in track. Turn right and proceed along the track. Shortly, Rainow comes into view over to the right. The track emerges on to a lane where the way is right to pass the three-storey farmhouse of Lower Brook Farm. The lane takes you back to the Robin Hood Inn and the car.

10 Woodbank
The Yacht Inn

The Yacht Inn is a listed building and can boast a long history. The lane at the side of the inn goes to Shotwick, just over 1 mile away. For centuries, before the river Dee silted up, Shotwick was a port. During these far-off days the Yacht Inn was a favourite with local sailors who would walk from Shotwick to quench their thirsts. Today, the inn offers an extremely wide choice of food and drink which can be consumed in a very attractively decorated setting and where large bay windows provide a bright ambience. Greenalls Local Bitter and Original Bitter are amongst the choices of available beer, together with Strongbow and Scrumpy Jack ciders.

The inn is a Millers Kitchen, resulting in a comprehensive choice of meals to suit every taste, served every day at lunchtime and during the evening. On Sundays a very reasonably priced traditional roast lunch is offered. The inn also has a specials board with between 20 and 30 different dishes to supplement the normal menu. A good choice of wines is also available. The inn has a beer garden and a play area for children.

Telephone: 01244 880216.

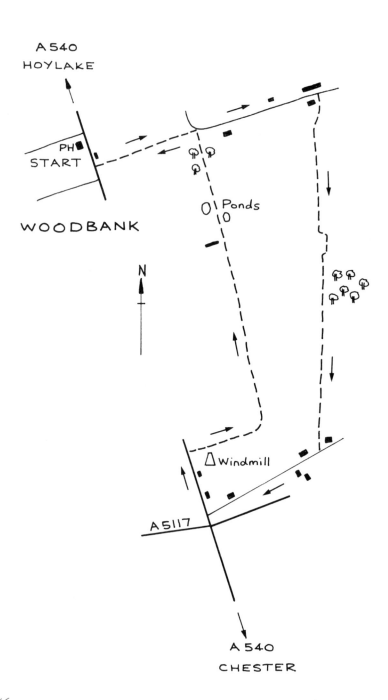

A 540
HOYLAKE

PH
START

WOODBANK

Ponds

N

Windmill

A 5117

A 540
CHESTER

How to get there: The A540 connects Chester with Hoylake on the Wirral peninsula. Four miles from Chester, and close to where the M56 currently terminates, the A540 cuts across the A5117. The Yacht Inn fronts on to the A540 1 mile from this intersection in the direction of Hoylake.

Parking: The inn has a large car park. Alternatively, there are a couple of roadside lay-bys in the vicinity.

Length of the walk: 3½ miles. Map: OS Landranger 117 Chester (GR 355731).

Although there are no major focal points to visit, this easy walk over the flat agricultural lands of the south Wirral presents an ideal opportunity to get away from it all. It is a walk where your stile-climbing abilities will be tested to the full, for there are 21 assorted devices to tackle before completing the journey back to the inn. Most of the route is along quiet field paths which provide a perfect platform for observing the local wildlife at close quarters.

The Walk
From the inn, cross the main road, and turn right to follow the pavement. Pass Hazels Farm and 60 metres further on go over a fence-stile on the left at the side of a gate. After 20 metres, pass over a stile at the side of a gateway to enter a large field. Walk forward now, keeping a hedgerow on the right about 30 metres away, to a stile visible at the side of a large tree across the field. Go over the stile, cross a short squat concrete plank-bridge and almost immediately cross another stile. Follow a footpath along the left-hand edge of the next field, keeping a hedgerow, which is interspersed with trees, on your immediate left. Cross a stile at the field corner and emerge at a bend in a crossing lane. There is a footpath which goes off down a track on the right here but ignore this and walk forward along the lane. After 150 metres pass School House Farm. A little further on there is a row of cottages on the left and Elm Cottage on the right, where there are boarding kennels.

Immediately on passing Elm Cottage, leave the lane to the right, and go over a plank-bridge and stile by the cottage garden hedgerow to enter a large field. Walk along the right-hand edge of the field, with a hedgerow on your immediate right. Keep by the hedgerow as it turns slightly to the right. At the field corner go over a stile at the side of a gate. Continue along the next field edge, still with a hedgerow on your immediate right. On reaching the field corner, go over a stile at the side of a gate. As before, follow the right-hand edge of the next field. At the field corner turn left at the facing hedge, and after 20 metres go over a stile on the right at the side of a gate. You have now entered a field of coarse grass at the far side of which can be seen a wood. Follow the hedgerow on the right as it kinks to the right and left, then go over a stile in a crossing fence.

You have now entered a wooded area. The main wood, Big Wood, is over to your left. This area abounds with all manner of wildlife where time can be spent observing the birds, squirrels and other creatures in their natural habitat.

Follow the facing path through the trees, that is, in the same general direction as before. Cross a stile and leave the trees behind to follow the right-hand edge of a field where there is a barbed-wire fence and a mixture of trees on the immediate right. Go over a stile at the side of a gate set in a crossing barbed-wire fence, and continue along the field edge. On reaching the field corner, go through a gate. After a further 30 metres, go over a stile at the side of a gate, and continue along the right-hand edge of a field in the general direction of a dwelling seen at the end of the field straight ahead. A stile at the field corner gives access to a path which takes you to the right of the dwelling and its garden shed. Arrive at a crossing lane, where the way is right.

A straight ¼ mile along the lane takes you to the Chester to Hoylake road. Turn right here and follow the roadside pavement. After ¼ mile, arrive at the entrance drive of Gibbet Windmill, a well-known landmark to travellers journeying to the Wirral. Immediately on passing the entrance drive, go over a stile on the right to enter a large field. Walk forward, keeping a hedgerow on your immediate right. About 50 metres past the windmill, there is a gate set in the hedgerow on the right. Go through the gate and continue in the same direction as before to walk along the edge of another large field but with the hedgerow now on your immediate left. Go over a stile and plank-bridge at the field corner. Walk forward and, after about 30 metres, turn left through a gate to enter a very long field at the end of which there is a row of single-storey outbuildings. The path follows the right-hand edge of this long field, where there is a hedgerow interspersed with trees on the immediate right. The path takes you towards the right-hand side of the outbuildings. On reaching the right-hand side of these follow a facing track which quickly takes you past ponds on right and left. At the field corner go through a facing gate. The track is hedged in now and emerges at a bend in a crossing lane. Go over a stile on the left here to follow the right-hand edge of a field. You are now back on part of the initial route. Follow the facing path, which leads back to the Chester to Hoylake road where you turn right for the short stroll back to the Yacht Inn.

Over Peover
Ye Olde Park Gate Inn

11

The name 'Peover' derives from the Anglo-Saxon 'Peeffer' – bright river. Unlike its counterpart, Lower Peover, Over Peover has no distinct village centre and is scattered over a wide area.

Built over 200 years ago, Ye Olde Park Gate Inn has remained predominantly unchanged except for an extensive growth of ivy which now envelops its front and gable walls. The inn was once a cobbler's shop and contains a large collection of old ladder-back Macclesfield chairs. Brass and copper utensils, hunting horns and old prints adorn the wood-panelled rooms. The majority of the beams are original and there are rustic brick fireplaces in every room. In the days when the inn provided refreshment for passing coach parties (the horse-drawn variety!) the landlord's wife would barbecue meat by employing spits which hung the meat over the open fireplaces.

The liquid refreshment is provided by Yorkshire's oldest brewery – Samuel Smith – famed for providing beer from the wood to the majority of its pubs. Draught cider is also available. The inn has built up an excellent reputation for its food and there is a wide selection to choose from, whether the requirement is for tasty sandwiches through to a substantial meal. A daily specials board proclaims other,

seasonal choices. Meals are served every lunchtime and evening. At the side of the inn there is an attractive garden with wooden tables and benches where children and well-behaved dogs are welcome.
Telephone: 01625 861455.

How to get there: The bulk of the scattered village of Over Peover lies between the A50 and A537 3 miles to the south-east of Knutsford. About 2½ miles to the south of Knutsford there is a sharp bend in the A50 close to the Whipping Stocks Inn. Leave the A50 at this point, drive past the inn, and continue for just over 1 mile to arrive at Ye Olde Park Gate Inn.

Parking: There is a car park at the side of the inn.

Length of the walk: 3½ miles. Map: OS Landranger 118 Stoke-on-Trent and Macclesfield (GR 785739).

The district has connections with the United States for, during the Second World War, General George Patton lived for a time at Peover Hall and his British HQ was at nearby Knutsford. Although Peover Hall is not open to the public, the walk will convey an impression of a tract of countryside that was so attractive to its founders. The walk is over level terrain and is easy going, making for an enjoyable evening stroll during the summer months when the days are long.

The Walk
On leaving the inn, turn right and follow the roadside footpath past Mainwaring Road. Sixty metres after the path finishes, and immediately on passing the entrance drive of Colshaw Hall, turn right to enter a signed bridleway. The track is enclosed by a wooden fence on the right and hedgerow on the left. After about 300 metres, leave the track to the left over a stile, where a footpath sign points across an extremely large field. A straight path of 250 metres leads to a farm approach track. Turn right now and follow the track away from the farm. After 100 metres the track becomes a macadam lane and leads over a deep dyke. After a further 100 metres there is a junction of ways. The way to the left goes to a farm, but keep right here and follow the lane to shortly pass through a gateway. On the right here is Lower Moss Wood, which is being developed as a nature reserve. The lane takes you past an isolated black and white cottage and then past Lower Mosswood House. A little further on, pass between a couple of facing dwellings – one of which is Ivy Old Cottage, and then 60 metres further on turn right to enter Percivals Lane.
 A straight ¼ mile leads to a T-junction, where the way is right. After 50 metres leave the lane and walk along a facing track which is headed

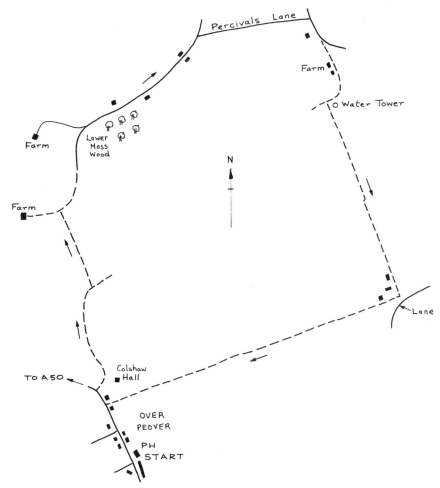

by a filled-in cattle grid and a gate. There is a bridleway sign here pointing along the track. Walk straight through the entrance gateway of Bowden Bank Farm to pass in front of an outbuilding with three doors set into the front of it. Follow a grassy track now which quickly turns to the right around a fenced-in compound where there is a pond (and usually an abundance of domestic fowl). On the left now is a tall, concrete water tower, a dominant landmark. Where the fencing enclosing the water tower finishes on the left there is a stile. Cross this, then quickly cross a second stile and continue forward along the edge of a large field with a fence, hedge, and trees on your immediate right.

At the field corner, go over a stile on the right and continue in the same direction as before with the fence, hedge and trees now on your immediate left. There is a large dwelling straight ahead to the right. Pass through a facing gate and walk past outbuildings. Where these outbuildings finish keep forward, still with the fence, hedge, and trees on your immediate left, to turn right 20 metres before arriving at a crossing lane. Go over a stile on the right here, to follow a narrow path where there is a mixture of trees on the left and a row of conifers on the right. A straight 100 metres leads to a stile (the large dwelling previously seen across the fields is on the immediate right here). On crossing the stile keep forward to follow a field edge. At the field corner go over another stile to enter open country. The path is in the same direction as before and follows the line of large widely spaced trees.

The route takes you over a farm approach drive via a couple of stiles, both of which are set at the side of gates. Continue in the same direction as before, keeping a fence on your immediate left. There are many newly planted trees in the vicinity. The path eventually leads to a stile at the side of a field gate with dwellings on both sides. Cross the stile to quickly arrive at a crossing road. Turn left now and follow the roadside footpath back to Ye Olde Park Gate Inn.

Allostock
The Drovers Arms Inn

The inn takes its name from the drovers who, during the late 18th and early 19th centuries, regularly brought cattle from the Welsh borders and Shropshire to auctions at Manchester. Records tell us that during the early 19th century, it cost ½ d per cow per night to stay in the field behind the inn.

The Drovers Arms is quite spacious and pictures on the walls remind us of its connections with droving. A fair range of liquid refreshment is available including Castle Eden Ale and other beers brewed by Boddingtons and Chester's. Draught cider can also be purchased. A comprehensive choice of food is on offer and the ever-changing specials board extends the choice still further. Upstairs is the Drovers Retreat, a small restaurant which can also be used for functions or as a family dining area. Food is available from 11 am to 10 pm every weekday and also at weekends. There is a large beer garden and an adjacent children's play area. The inn also has a bowling green.

Telephone: 01565 722255.

How to get there: The A50 connects Knutsford with Holmes Chapel. The Drovers Arms fronts on to this road 4 miles from Knutsford.

Parking: There is a car park at the side of the inn.

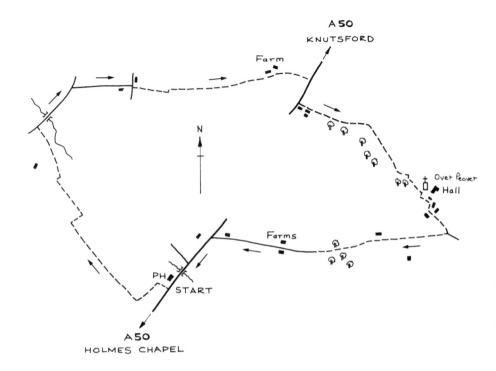

Length of the walk: 4½ miles. Map: OS Landranger 118 Stoke-on-Trent and Macclesfield (GR 755728).

Although, technically, the Drovers Arms Inn is in the parish of Allostock, the majority of the walk is through the parish of Peover Superior and during the first mile of today's walk you will never be too far away from the winding water of the Peover Eye stream. After crossing agricultural land the route takes you through Peover Park to the church of St Lawrence and on past Peover Hall. The return leg is via lanes and wooded tracks.

The Walk

A footpath commences close by the entrance to the car park where a footpath sign points away from the A50 towards Lower Peover. Go through a gate here to enter a field. Walk forward, keeping a hedge on your immediate right, then turn left after 50 metres to follow the field edge. After 150 metres go through a gate on the right. The footpath runs straight across the next field to the field corner; however, there may be a diversion here taking you around the edge of the field. Go over a stile at the field corner and almost immediately pass over a

54

second stile set between bushes. Turn left here to proceed along a field edge, keeping a hedgerow on your immediate left. Walk along the edge of three fields and cross a number of stiles en route. On emerging from the third field there is no longer a hedgerow on the left. Turn right here and proceed along a field edge with a hedgerow now on your right. At the field corner go over a stile in a crossing fence and turn left. Follow a grassy path which stays parallel with the fence on your left and after 250 metres turn right at a facing hedgerow. After only 20 metres go left through bushes to emerge into a field through a gap in a crossing fence. A delightful thatched dwelling can be seen about 150 metres away across the field straight ahead.

A well-defined footpath on the right generally follows the course of the Peover Eye stream which meanders along on the right here. The stubby tower of Lower Peover church comes into view shortly across the fields. This pleasant path emerges on a lane via a stile in a crossing hedgerow. Turn right and follow Foxcovert Lane over Peover Eye. The lane climbs between grassy banks, then after 200 metres there is a junction of lanes. Turn right here to enter Mill Lane. After ¼ mile, arrive at a junction with Free Green Lane. Cross this lane diagonally to the right and go over a stile at the side of a gate. A short section of track takes you to another stile. On crossing this stile you have entered a large, rough, undulating field. Walk forward, bearing slightly left, and cross the field to arrive at a stile in a crossing hedge. This stile is about 20 metres to the right of a staggered corner in the facing hedgerow and is set between a Scots pine and a couple of oak trees. On crossing this stile turn left, and then right, to follow a field edge, keeping a hedgerow on your immediate left. Pass through a gateway at the field corner to follow a well-defined track across the next field. Pass through a facing gate and continue along the track, keeping a hedgerow on your left. The track takes you through another gate, at which point you are approaching a farm you will see about 100 metres away. Walk to the right of the farm and on past a wooden gate on the left over which can be seen a circular display of flowers in the centre of a turning circle for vehicles. Just a few metres further on go over a metal fence on the left where a short section of the top bar has been removed to provide access. Walk between farm outbuildings to turn right on to a gravel drive which takes you over a cattle grid and leads away from the farm. On the left here, is the entrance gate of Hillcrest House. A further 200 metres along the drive takes you to a crossing road.

Go over the road, taking care as it is usually quite busy, and turn right to follow the roadside footpath. After 150 metres turn left by Nixon's Cottage, where footpath signs point away from the road; one of these signs indicates 'Over Peover Church'. After 30 metres keep to the left of Tree Tops and follow a path which quickly takes you over a stile to enter a large field. Walk forward now, keeping a hedge, fence and trees on your immediate right. Go over a crossing place in a fence at the field corner close by a small derelict brick building. Turn right here and walk across a rough, open, tract of grassland, keeping trees about 60 metres away on your right. Arrive at a stile set in a fence to the left of a facing wood. Cross the stile and after 20 metres turn right over another stile which gives access to the wood. Follow an obvious track between the trees and keep forward past a breach in the trees on the right leading to ornamental gates you will see about 150 metres away. Bear right to follow a stony track that takes you through overhanging trees and to the left of an outbuilding. Keep to the left now and walk towards the church of St Lawrence, Over Peover, which comes into view straight ahead. This approach is through an avenue of overhanging and intertwining trees. The church contains some fine relics and alabaster effigies, the earliest of which dates from 1415, of the Mainwaring family. Over the wall at the side of the church, is Over Peover Hall. The original hall was constructed entirely of timber, but this was pulled down in 1585 and a new brick building constructed during the following two years. It is not open to the public.

Follow a flagged path away from the church. The way is now to the left, but first of all take a look at the pets' graveyard on the right, where the favourite animals of the Mainwaring family are buried. An interesting sundial is close by. Turn left after leaving the church, as directed, soon to pass a rather ornate gate which is on the left. Turn right and then left to pass close to the old stables. These stables, erected in 1656, contain carved Jacobean woodwork and have ornamental plaster ceilings. Pass through a gateway and at the junction ahead turn right to follow a rough macadam drive. A straight 250 yards takes you to St Anthony's Cottages. Go through a small gate here and continue along a grassy path. After a further 150 metres keep forward through a gap in a metal fence. The way is partly cobbled here, and leads through trees, then becomes a track between hedgerows. Emerge on to a facing lane. There is a market garden on the left here, but keep forward along the facing lane shortly to pass between farms. A straight ¼ mile leads to London Lodge, shortly after which a crossing road is met. Turn left now and follow the roadside footpath. Over to the right here is Peover Old Farm, renovated to good effect.

Cross the road, with care, and continue along the opposite footpath. Pass the head of Free Green Lane. A further 300 metres and you are back at the Drovers Arms Inn and the car.

Hatchmere
The Carriers Inn

In an idyllic setting close by the still waters of Hatchmere lake, the Carriers Inn has been in existence for over 300 years. Its name relates to the wagoners or carriers who used to stop here on their way to the port of Frodsham with agricultural produce, salt, cheese and other wares for loading onto sailing ships and barges.

The inn is roomy, having a split-level lounge with highly varnished timbers presenting a pleasing appearance and where choices from the full range of Burtonwood ales can be consumed in comfort. Draught Woodpecker and Strongbow ciders are also available. Meals are served every day at lunchtime and during the evening. A 'Special Sunday Roast' extends the choice at weekends. The menu is changed on a daily basis and offers many diverse special dishes as well as the more traditional steaks, lamb, beef, turkey and gammon. Seafood dishes are usually on the menu together with various sandwiches and salads. The gardens at the rear of the inn lead down to Hatchmere lake. There is also a garden area where children can play.

Telephone: 01928 788258.

How to get there: The B5152 connects Frodsham with the A556 near Delamere. About 4½ miles from Frodsham and 2½ miles from Delamere, is the attractive lakeside village of Hatchmere. The Carriers Inn fronts on to the B5152 only metres from the water's edge.

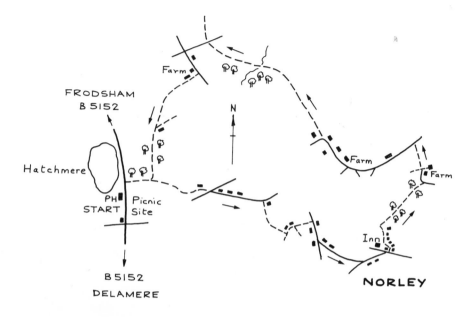

Parking: There is a car park at the side of the inn; alternatively a large public car park and picnic area are almost opposite the inn.

Length of the walk: 4½ miles. Map: OS Landranger 117 Chester (GR 554722).

Delamere Forest covers about 4,000 acres of rolling Cheshire countryside. One of the most attractive locations within the forest's boundaries is the lovely reed-fringed pool at Hatchmere. Apart from offering an opportunity to relax by the waterside this walk presents a chance to explore a little further into the surrounding countryside. There is a visit to the forest village of Norley and this, coupled with a mixture of tracks, paths and lanes combines to offer a most rewarding excursion.

The Walk
On leaving the inn turn left, cross the road and enter a tree-lined track where a footpath sign points towards Norley Road and School Lane. After 120 metres, the track bends to the left, but walk forward here to follow a narrow path which is headed by a sign pointing to School Lane. The path leads through ferns and trees and emerges on to a gravel track. Keep forward along the track and then continue past another which goes off to the left. Arrive at the junction of School Lane and Post Office Lane. Enter Post Office Lane and continue along

58

the laneside pavement. Where the pavement peters out keep forward and gently descend along the lane.

Leave the lane to the right now, just before a house on the right is reached, and enter a narrow hedged-in path which commences at the left-hand side of an electricity pole. After 100 metres go over a stile and emerge into a sloping field. Keep to the right now, along the higher ground, with a tall unruly hedge on your right. At the field corner, go over a stile and then turn left to follow a track. Pass close to dwellings, then keep forward, ignoring a track which goes off to the right. The facing track takes you to a crossing road. Go over the road and turn right to follow the roadside pavement. On the right is Norley village hall, but turn left now to enter Maddocks Hill. On the immediate right at this point is Norley Central Methodist church.

On reaching the bottom of Maddocks Hill, enter School Bank and follow the roadside pavement in the direction of Crowton and Northwich. Shortly, over to the left, the Tiger's Head Inn comes into view. A little further on there is a dwelling on the left called Rose Cottage. Enter a narrow path which commences at the side of this dwelling. There are modern buildings on the right here and the path skirts around their gardens. On the left is the bowling green of the Tiger's Head Inn. Follow the path as it winds and cross a couple of stiles. The path now takes you along the edge of a large garden which slopes up to the right and is mainly laid to lawn. Gradually descend to the corner of this garden and arrive at a facing stile. Do not cross this but turn right and climb along the edge of the garden boundary. After only 20 metres bear to the left where a footpath has been cut out of the side of an embankment. A well-defined path takes you through trees, and keeps on top of a woody knoll, where there are a couple of vertical footpath signs pointing the way. The path then follows the edge of a large field.

At the field corner enter a facing grassy track where there are trees on both sides. A stile at the side of a gate takes you on to a lane, where the way is left. After 50 metres there is a farm on the right. Walk straight across the farm approach drive and almost immediately go over a facing stile where there is a footpath sign close by. You have now entered a large field. Keep forward and cross the field, aiming to the right of a large tree about 150 metres away straight ahead. On crossing the field go over a fence-stile by the side of a gate and enter a lane where the way is left. Gradually climb along the lane. At the top of the climb pass three charming dwellings, Four Winds, The Cottage and Wayside. A little further on pass the entrance drive of Westwood and continue past a lane on the left which goes to Home Farm. On meeting a junction of lanes, turn right at the post box to enter Town Farm Lane. Pass the attractive buildings of Town Farm and keep on past The Paddock. Where the lane turns to the left keep forward to enter a facing hedged-in track between The Oranges and a dwelling on the right constructed in 1697. Almost immediately the track forks. Ignore the turning to the right and keep forward shortly to pass by a large modern dwelling which is on the right. The track shortly takes you into a large field. Continue forward now, in the same general direction as before, and follow the field edge, keeping a hedgerow which is interspersed with trees on your immediate left. There are long views to the right across the Weaver valley.

On approaching the field corner the path begins to descend. Go over a stile at the field corner and arrive at a crossing track. Turn right, but after only 10 metres, leave the track to the left and descend down a rough grassy slope. On reaching the bottom of the descent bear left and go through a small wooden gate where a wooden plank has been set at ground level to enable walkers to traverse a stream.

Care is now required in order not to miss the path. On going through the gate there is a heavily wooded fenced-in area on the left. After only a few metres bear right and climb to the top of a grassy embankment. At the top you have entered a rough, but generally level, field. On the immediate left there is a fenced-in wooded area sloping down to your left. Walk forward now, keeping parallel with the fence on your left, and walk to a stile you will see about 100 metres away in a crossing fence. Go over this stile and walk forward across the next field to a stile at the left side of a field gate about 150 metres away. The stile gives access to a lane where the way is left. A straight 150 metres along the lane takes you to crossroads. Tun left now and walk along the grass verge on the right-hand side of the road.

After about 300 metres walk past Brownmoss Farm on the right. Immediately on passing the farm turn right to proceed along a concrete driveway, where a footpath sign points towards Hatchmere and School Lane. The driveway takes you along the side of farm outbuildings. Pass through the smaller of two facing gates. The concrete finishes now but the way is forward along a grassy track where there is a fence on the right and hedgerow on the left. The track leads into a field via a gate. Follow the right hand edge of the field keeping a fence on your immediate right. At the field corner there is a choice of gate or stile. A fenced-in path emerges onto a track close by a dwelling. Keep forward here, in the direction of Hatchmere. After 250 metres the track bends to the right. A straight 120 metres takes you to a crossing road close by the Carriers Inn.

14 Bottom-of-the Oven
The Stanley Arms

Many years ago, the Stanley Arms sat at the side of the main road to Buxton. Following alterations to the route of the A537, the inn is now located in a rather remote spot with the majority of through traffic passing by. However, this very remoteness is a source of attraction for ramblers and cyclists because there are some lovely views of the surrounding hills from the inn, which was previously a farm belonging to the curiously named hamlet of Bottom-of-the-Oven.

Fresh flowers decorate the rooms at all times and during the summer months there is usually a magnificent outside display of flowers. The inn, which is owned by Marston's, provides a good range of beers including real ale favourites such as Burton Bitter and Pedigree. Although it is small, the Stanley Arms has built up quite a reputation for its food, be it from the bar, or in the small restaurant. Meals are served every lunchtime and in the evening and a wide choice is on offer. There is also a board proclaiming daily specials. The inn has a family room, a beer-garden and an outdoor garden area where children are welcome.

Telephone: 01260 252414.

How to get there: The winding A537 links Macclesfield with Buxton. About 5 miles from Macclesfield a secondary road leaves the A537 in a southerly direction, where a sign tells you that Wildboarclough is 3 miles away. Drive along this road and, after ¾ mile, arrive at the Stanley Arms.

Parking: There is a car park at the inn. Alternatively, limited parking is usually available at Forest Chapel.

Length of the walk: 3¾ miles. Map: OS Landranger 118 Stoke-on-Trent and Macclesfield (GR 980724).

This walk is entirely within the Peak District National Park, where the effort of climbing is rewarded with magnificent views across miles of rolling countryside. This hilly district in the east of the county completely contradicts any argument that Cheshire is a flat county. The outward journey is along tracks and involves a climb to Forest Chapel. The walk continues along the fringes of Macclesfield Forest from where there are long views to Shining Tor, Windgather Rocks and Kerridge Hill. The return leg takes you through a lush valley and rewards you with views of the pointed peak of Shutlingsloe – which has been described as the Matterhorn of the Peak District.

The Walk
From the inn, turn right and then left to walk along a road in the direction of Forest Chapel, Wildboarclough and Wincle. Pass Chambers Farm, then turn next right in the direction of Forest Chapel (½ mile). Enter a track on the right now, which begins opposite Forest Lodge. The track is stony and climbs quite steeply at first although the going soon becomes much easier. It leads to Forest Chapel, a simple little church erected in 1673 and rebuilt during 1834. The church is well known for its annual Rushbearing Service, held on the first Sunday after 12th August each year.

Shortly after passing the church, there is a junction of ways. Our route is to the right where a track climbs at the side of Toot Hill House; a sign here says 'Forest Walk'. However, before entering this track it is worth walking forward for a few metres to admire long views over Macclesfield Forest.

Follow the track as directed. There is a footpath on the left shortly, which goes to Walker Barn, but ignore this and climb forward along the track. There are trees on the left now. At the top of the climb an electrical reflector mast is set in a clearing on the left. The views from this spot are excellent. With the mast at your back you can look straight across the valley to the rolling hill of Shining Tor almost 2 miles away. During the summer months hang-gliders and para-gliders

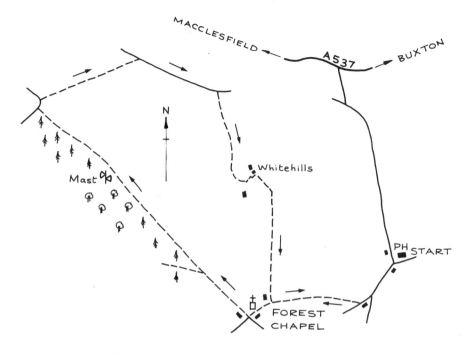

are usually to be seen near the summit.

To the right of Shining Tor, on the skyline, you will see the Cat and Fiddle Inn which, at over 1,600 ft, is the second highest inn in England. Well to the left of Shining Tor perhaps you can make out the crags of Windgather Rocks, where apprentice rock-climbers learn their trade.

The track descends now, and leads to a T-junction at a crossing lane. Straight ahead, to the right, you should be able to see White Nancy at the far end of Kerridge Hill; there are also long views out across the Cheshire Plain. Turn right; the lane immediately turns to the left, but leave the lane here through a gate on the right. Walk over a short stretch of concrete and quickly pass through a second gate to enter a large rough sloping field. There is a stone wall which descends to your left and another which gradually ascends to your right. Bisect both of these walls by walking diagonally to your left to cross rough, open, ground. There is a faint path here which gradually converges with a gully on the right. At the field corner go through a gate to emerge on a road. Turn right, and after ¼ mile, leave the road to the right to enter a drive where a sign indicates Whitehills Farm. Cross a cattle grid and continue along the drive. If the day is clear a splendid panorama unfolds ahead towards the pointed peak of Shutlingsloe.

Follow the drive as it descends and turns to the left, taking you towards outbuildings. Pass through a gate about 40 metres before the outbuildings and, after a further 20 metres, go over a stile on the right to follow a straight stretch of path between fences close to a large outbuilding covered with asbestos sheets. Turn right, and then left, to skirt around the outbuilding, then go over a stile. There is another stile here, in the opposite fence, but do not cross this. Instead, turn right and continue, keeping the fence on your immediate left. A hawthorn hedge some 20 metres away on your right runs parallel with the fence on your left. Straight ahead you will see a pair of facing metal gates, both of which are somewhat rusty. Go through the left-hand gate and walk forward for only 10 metres or so, to turn right over a stile. Descend along the edge of a rough field in the direction of Shutlingsloe, which can be seen straight ahead. There is a hawthorn hedge on the right here. At the bottom of the descent cross a stream and fence-stile to ascend along the facing field edge, keeping a fence and stone wall on your immediate right. Go over a couple of stiles at the top of the climb and follow a well-defined path taking you to the left of a farm. Descend steps to arrive at a crossing track close to the church of Forest Chapel which you passed earlier.

Turn left and retrace your original route, turn left at the crossing road and then left again to arrive back at the Stanley Arms.

15 Shakerley Mere
The Three Greyhounds

In an area where farming is a way of life, it is perhaps not too surprising to learn that the Three Greyhounds was originally a farm. Its strategic location at the junction of two former drove roads, one between Northwich and Congleton and the other between Knutsford and Middlewich, made an ideal site for an inn where weary travellers could take a break from their journeying to rest and refresh themselves. A familiar feature to these travellers of yesteryear would have been the 250 year old yew tree that stands in front of the inn.

The Three Greyhounds has a spacious and comfortable lounge where a range of Greenalls Whitley beers, draught cider, and cooked lunches are provided. The inn has built up a good reputation for its home-cooked pies – the meat and potato and steak and Guinness varieties being particular favourites. Other specialities include a selection of triple toasted sandwiches. If the weather is favourable, visitors have the option of taking their refreshment on a number of picnic tables situated on a grassed area at the side of the inn and where children are welcome. Well-behaved dogs are permitted in the taproom.

Telephone: 01565 722234.

65

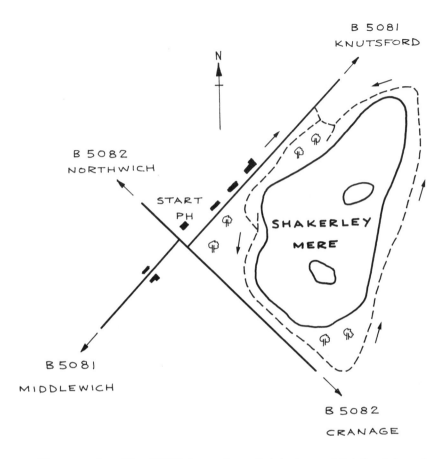

How to get there: The B5081 is used as a link between Middlewich and Knutsford. Close to where the road passes over the M6 there is a staggered junction with the B5082. The Three Greyhounds is situated near this junction on the B5082 road.

Parking: There are generous parking facilities at the pub. Alternatively, car parking is available at Shakerley Mere.

Length of the walk: 1½ miles. Map: OS Landranger 118 Stoke-on-Trent and Macclesfield (GR 730710).

A simple short walk around Shakerley Mere Nature Reserve is one which gives tremendous pleasure to nature lovers. The mere and surrounding woodland support a diverse range of wildlife and each season presents an ever-changing scene. The

66

woodlands are host to most of the familiar species of bird, whilst Canada geese, mallard, heron, mute swans and black-headed gulls are a common sight on the waters of the mere. Cormorants fly to these waters from their coastal breeding grounds to feed on the fish, and more exotic visitors arrive at different times of the year. Heather thrives in the area and the heathland is of recognised importance and designated as a site of botanical interest. Fishermen can pit their skills against carp, bream, perch and the predatory pike. Although the walk is short in terms of distance, it is long in interest as there is so much to see and learn. Information boards provide a wealth of detail relating to the development of the site and the wildlife connected with it. You will arrive back at the car with the impression that your journey was far in excess of 1½ miles.

The Walk

On leaving the Three Greyhounds turn left, and then immediately left again, to follow a roadside footpath. After 250 metres arrive at one of the entrances to Shakerley Mere Nature Reserve. There are a number of alternative walks which could be undertaken, although it is probably best to keep to a set configuration.

Enter the site, and turn immediately to your right to follow a path where a sign indicates 'Woodland Path'. This takes you through trees, over a wooden footbridge, and then joins a broad path which runs alongside the mere. The mere was formed after large excavations were carried out to recover a particular type of sand which was then used in the manufacture of coloured glass. The ensuing hole was then filled with water and the surrounding area subsequently landscaped. A number of islands were also constructed.

The path takes you away from the water's edge for a short distance and then turns to the left to run parallel with the M6. On reaching the head of the mere the path turns to the left and leads back to the entrance gate. Leave the site at this point and retrace your original route back to the Three Greyhounds.

Oakgrove
16 The Fool's Nook Inn

The Fool's Nook Inn has refreshed travellers, both on the road and from the adjoining canal, for over 160 years. The origin of its unusual name causes much local argument. Some say that because the inn lies close to a rather severe bend (or nook) in the road, which some drivers approach far too quickly, the name fool's nook seems quite appropriate; others argue that the name refers to a meeting place for merrymakers, otherwise known as fools. Whatever the reason for its name, the inn we see today is well known for the quality of its food, its beer, and its friendly service.

The Fool's Nook contains some well-polished brassware and furniture from a bygone age. Boddingtons beers are served and the comprehensive menu offers a wide choice. Sandwiches, light meals and main courses are available every lunchtime and evening and there is a selection to suit the most discerning of palates. Apart from the traditional soup of the day, prawn cocktail and pâté, there are more interesting starters including Chinese dim-sum, prawns cooked in the Japanese style and deep-fried crabmeat parcels. The main courses are just as varied with home-made steak pie, lasagne (both verdi and vegetable), steak, fish, gammon, roast ham, scampi, chicken (breast, tikka and curried), lamb rogan josh, salads and a hearty ploughman's platter. Special dishes of the day are usually on offer, together with a good choice of sweets. A patio garden area at the rear of the inn is ideal for families, where children and well-behaved dogs are most welcome.

Telephone: 01260 252254.

How to get there: The A523 connects Macclesfield with Leek. The Fool's Nook Inn fronts on to this road at Oakgrove, 3 miles to the south of Macclesfield.

Parking: The inn has a large car park for patrons. Alternatively, there is some limited parking space available down the lane which begins opposite the inn close to the canal swing bridge.

Length of the walk: 3½ miles. Map: OS Landranger 118 Stoke-on-Trent and Macclesfield (GR 918695).

Today's walk has a watery flavour. The first 2 miles follow the course of the Macclesfield Canal – whilst during the latter stages Sutton Reservoir is visited. In between, field paths, which never venture far from bubbling streams, lead both to and from the interesting village of Sutton Lane Ends. The walk returns to Oakgrove along a winding country lane.

The Walk

Cross the road in front of the Fool's Nook Inn and go over a low-level swing bridge to cross the Macclesfield Canal. Turn immediately right to walk along the canal towpath. The canal runs parallel to the main road at first and then gradually turns away to the left.

The canal was first opened for traffic on 10th November 1831 and connects the Trent and Mersey Canal, near Kidsgrove, with the Peak Forest Canal at Marple. In its prime the Macclesfield Canal transported cargoes of coal, salt, lime and stone. Today it provides a basis for leisure pursuits, used by boat people, walkers and bird-watchers. It was in this very area that the famous canal builder James Brindley served his apprenticeship before going on to produce his civil engineering masterpieces, the best known of which was the Bridgewater Canal.

The canal runs close to the railway for a short distance and then gently turns to the right passing under bridge 46. After bridge 45 there are fields on both sides and long views to the hills of Macclesfield Forest straight ahead. At the next bridge (44) leave the canal towpath and walk over the bridge. Shortly after the entrance drive of Sutton Hall (Hotel) turn next left to enter a broad track at the side of a

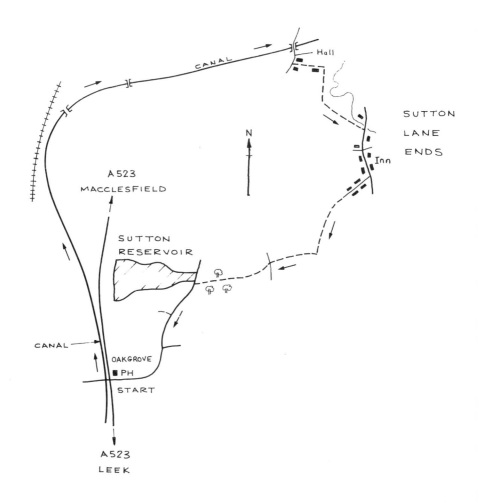

bungalow; a sign here indicates 'Sutton Hall Farm'. On passing the next house (Sutton Seate) turn right and pass through a gate to enter a field. Keep a hedge on your left side and after 50 metres go over a fence stile on the left. With the stile at your back walk forward, bearing right, aiming to the right of a dwelling about 150 metres away. Pass close to the winding water of Rossendale Brook (which is a tributary of the river Bollin), then go over a stile to continue along a waterside path. Emerge on a road in the village of Sutton Lane Ends. Turn right and follow the roadside footpath.

The village contains a number of interesting stone cottages, no doubt once inhabited by workers involved with the silk industry which was started in nearby Langley during the early years of the 19th century. Alas, the industry is no more for the Langley works closed in 1964 resulting in a change of identity for the surrounding villages. New housing has also brought changes to the area although the nucleus of the village has altered little over the years.

On passing the Lamb Inn turn right to enter Symondley Road. At the end of the road enter a field through a gap at the side of a gate. Continue along the right-hand edge of two fields and pass over two stiles; after crossing the second stile your way is at right angles to the previous route. The path now goes along the top of a bank where a brook runs close by. At a crossing driveway go over a bridge and continue in the same direction as before to follow a well-worn path by the brook. The path takes you through a gap in a fence, through trees, and over a wooden footbridge to emerge on a lane close to Sutton Reservoir. This is an attractive place to linger for a while as there is usually an abundance of wildlife to observe.

Turn left and climb along the lane away from the reservoir. Pass a private drive which goes to Broadoak Farm then follow the lane along more level terrain. Shortly, the lane descends then turns to the right to become Radcliffe Road. A few more strides and you are back at the Fool's Nook.

Swettenham
The Swettenham Arms

17

The tiny village of Swettenham sits on the north bank of the river Dane in the heart of rich agricultural land. The village has changed little over many years and rewards the visitor with scenes of pastoral splendour.

Tucked away behind the village church, the Swettenham Arms is a delightful country inn which can boast a long and varied history. Although the majority of the heavily timbered building that we see today dates from the 16th century, the origins of the inn reach even further back into the past. From as early as the 13th century the site was occupied by a nunnery which, amongst its other functions, catered for funeral parties attending burials at the nearby church. Perhaps these activities were responsible for the eventual change of the site to licensed premises.

Visitors to the inn will discover a warm, friendly and informal atmosphere. The landlord and his wife ensure that high standards of quality are maintained and provide imaginatively prepared English cooking at sensible prices together with a choice of superbly kept real ales, fine wines and malt whiskies. Meals are served every day at lunchtime and in the evenings and a wide choice is presented. House

specialities include a tasty steak, kidney and mushroom pie, rib of steak in pepper sauce, succulent tender chicken, roast beef and various seafood dishes. The inn has a beer garden and a garden area for children.
Telephone: 01477 571284.

How to get there: Swettenham is situated 2½ miles due east of Holmes Chapel and is about 3 miles by road from Twemlow Green and the A535. The Swettenham Arms is located at the rear of the village church.

Parking: There is a huge car park in front of the Swettenham Arms.

Length of the walk: 3 miles. Map: OS Landranger 118 Stoke-on-Trent and Macclesfield (GR 800672).

Life just ambles along here and to stroll amongst the gentle ripples of the surrounding landscape is an ideal way to relax. The outward part of the walk takes you by Kermincham Hall, whilst the return leg has an abundance of field paths and stiles.

The Walk

On leaving the car park, turn left in front of the church where a grassy path takes you to a stile. Cross the stile and follow a field edge, keeping a fence on your immediate right. Over to the right is a splendid brick and timber house. A couple of stiles close to outbuildings give access to a narrow lane. Turn right and then left to descend along a rough lane. Cross Midge Brook, then, after climbing for a further 40 metres, go over a stile on the left which takes you into a rough hillside field. Cross a wooden plank-bridge, bear right, and climb to go over a stile which is set close to a field gate. Turn left to follow a track and shortly go through a gate, then a second gate close to a farmhouse, where the track has become a macadam lane. Follow the lane through farm outbuildings. It then turns to the right where Jodrell Bank Telescope comes into view straight ahead. On reaching buildings follow the lane as it turns sharply to the left, then bear right, and descend past a pond. Sitting on a rise on the left is the imposing building of Kermincham Hall. Follow the lane for almost ½ mile and emerge on a crossing road. Turn right.

After ¼ mile, and after passing a large dwelling called Rowley Lodge, leave the roadside over a stile on the right where a footpath sign points to Swettenham. Walk forward across a rough field to converge gradually with a wall you will see straight ahead. Go over a stile at the field corner which is set next to this old wall, which

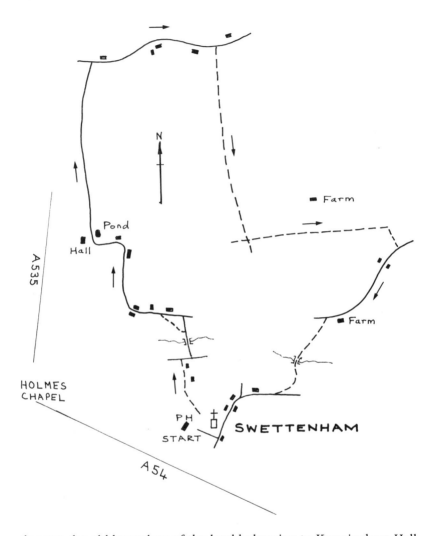

denotes the old boundary of the land belonging to Kermincham Hall.

The path hugs the wall across the next field. Drop down into a hollow at the field corner and cross over a stile. The path gradually leads away from the wall now and takes you to a stile about 150 metres away at the side of a field gate. On crossing the stile there is a junction of paths. Turn left here to follow a field edge keeping a fence and hedge on your immediate left. The path follows the next two field edges and takes you over two stiles; 80 metres after crossing the second stile go over a double stile on the left and continue in the same general direction as before, but now with a fence and trees on your right. After crossing another stile at the field corner the path has turned to the right, still following a field edge, and leads to a crossing lane. Turn right along the lane which takes you past Cross Lane Farm. Follow the lane as it bends to the right. Pass close by a farm, after which the lane has become a track, then 100 metres after passing the farm there is a stile on the left from where you have a view of Swettenham village across the valley.

Go over this stile and descend along a well-worn path. The area is kept as a nature reserve and we are asked to protect the surroundings by avoiding damage or disturbance to plants and other wildlife. Cross a stout wooden footbridge taking you over Midge Brook and keep to the left of bushes. Climb along the left edge of an undulating field. Near the top of the climb bear right and walk to a stile which gives access to a lane where the way is right. You are now on the route back to the Swettenham Arms.

18 Duddon
The Headless Woman Inn

Duddon was once at the very edge of Delamere Forest which in medieval times covered a vast area of the Cheshire countryside. However, the ensuing deforestation has created an area of rolling countryside overlooked and protected by the adjacent Willington hills. This cosy village, with its charming cottages and scattered smallholdings, was once at the centre of a thriving farming community, with the majority of residents working on the farms and living in tied cottages. Although farming is still important, many of the present-day dwellings are owned by people who earn their livings away from the village.

The Headless Woman Inn derives its name from the story of a maid who worked at nearby Hockenhull Hall. She was approached by Cromwell's troops during the Civil War and asked to reveal the hiding place of her employer's jewellery. When she refused, the soldiers tortured and then beheaded her. She is still reputed to walk between the inn and Hockenhull Hall, so keep a sharp eye open on this walk! During the 1930s the landlord, a Captain Clayton, placed a figure from the stern of a ship in the garden of the inn. This effigy of a headless woman was a well-known landmark to those passing the inn; unfortunately, it was stolen a number of years ago.

The inn's comfortable and cosy lounge, has low beams and an abundance of brasses. A range of Greenalls Whitley beers is available and draught cider may be purchased. A wide choice of good-value food is on offer and diners have the option of eating bar snacks in the lounge or using a small adjacent restaurant. Meals are served every lunchtime and evening and there is always variety with a specials board proclaiming tasty alternatives to the more traditional set menus. At the side of the inn there is a beer garden and an amusement area for children. The landlord allows well-behaved dogs in the garden area but not inside the inn.
Telephone: 01829 781252.

How to get there: Duddon straddles the A51 midway between Tarporley and Tarvin. The Headless Woman Inn fronts on to this road in the centre of the village.

Parking: There is a large car park at the side of the inn.

Length of the walk: 3½ miles. Map: OS Landranger 117 Chester (GR 512648).

The walk is easy going and, once outside the perimeter of the village, a combination of field paths and country lanes take you through a peaceful rural locality.

The Walk
On leaving the inn, walk across the grassed area close to the children's amusements, then go through a gap in a hedgerow to enter a lane. Turn right and walk along Back Lane. Pass Greenacres and Laurel Park, to arrive at a T-junction, where the way is right. On the left now is the fine black and white building of Duddon Old Hall, which has belonged to the same family for generations. A straight 80 metres takes you to the main road. Turn left here in the direction of Nantwich and follow the roadside footpath. Pass the small brick building of St Peter's church and its adjacent school. After a further 200 metres there is a roadside farm on the left, also a small postbox here. Turn left immediately on passing the farm to enter a grassy track leading away from the road. This track commences almost opposite a mock black and white farm building on the other side of the road. A straight 80 metres takes you to a field gate. Go over a stile at the side of the gate and walk forward to descend along a large, rough field. Two field gates can be seen shortly, straight ahead. Go through the right-hand gate, there is a wooden plank-bridge that crosses a dyke here. Climb up the facing field in the same direction as before. The path reaches more level terrain, then takes you to the left of a large isolated tree

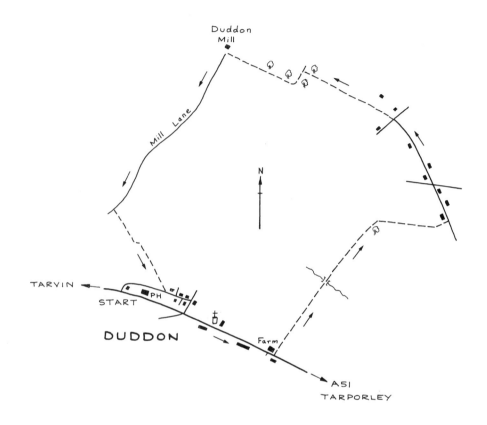

about 15 metres before the end of the field is reached. Go over a facing fence to enter a large undulating field. (When I passed this way the top section of fence was removable allowing you to step over a couple of strands of low-set barbed wire.) Turn diagonally right now and walk to the field corner, which is about 250 metres away. A gate at the field corner gives access to a short length of track taking you to a lane at the side of Laburnum Cottage. Turn left, pass in front of the cottage, and continue along the lane.

Pass The Haven and continue to a crossroads. Go straight over the crossing road and walk along the facing lane. Pass The Beeches and Pembroke House to arrive at another crossing road. Walk straight over this and enter a facing hedged-in grassy track. There is an attractive detached modern dwelling on the right here. After 200 metres a stile at the side of a gate gives access to a very large field. Keep forward across the field, in the same direction as the track you have just left, and walk towards trees which you will see 250 metres away across the field. Go over a combined footbridge and stile at the end of the field and emerge on a track, where the way is left. After 70 metres follow the track as it turns to the right. There is a tall hedge of trees and conifers on the right now, and on the left a rough, sloping field. After a further 250 metres the track takes you on to a lane close by a farm which is on the site of the ancient Duddon Mill, where the waters of the common brook were utilised to turn the old mill wheel. Fruit is now the mainstay crop of the present farm.

Turn left and follow the lane away from the farm. This pleasant lane winds between high-banked hedges. After ½ mile leave the lane to the left, over a stile at the side of a gate, where a footpath sign points towards Duddon. Follow a path along a field edge – keeping a hedgerow on your immediate right. After 80 metres arrive at the field corner. There is an ornate stile on the right here, but ignore this and keep forward to go over a stile at the field corner close by a gate. Continue, as before, and after 70 metres go over another stile by a gate, then turn diagonally left to pass over a stile in a crossing fence. Continue in the same general direction as before, keeping a hedgerow on your immediate right. After a further 200 metres pass through a wide gap in a crossing hedge, then walk forward to arrive at the field corner some 30 metres to the right of a dwelling which can be seen straight ahead. Go over a stile at the field corner and enter a lane. Turn right and walk back to the Headless Woman Inn.

19 Christleton
The Plough Inn

Christleton has had a long and chequered history, contains many fine buildings and is an interesting place through which to meander.

The Plough, actually at Brown Heath a little east of Christleton, was originally a farmhouse dating back to 1750, at which time it is known that a gallows stood at the adjacent crossroads. The farmhouse evolved into an inn when permission was given for local farmhands to quench their thirsts at the premises. Until 1959 the inn was only licensed to sell beer, stout and cider; however, today's choice of liquid refreshment is much wider. A range of Greenalls ales is available and the inn is one of a small number of outlets where the increasingly popular Young's of London ale can be purchased. Meals are served every day between 12 noon and 2 pm and a good selection is on offer. There is a choice of soups, and hot dishes include chilli, moussaka, lasagne, seafood lasagne, various filled pancakes and vegetarian dishes, and a daily specials board greatly extends the available choice. Sweets include hot chocolate fudge cake, apple pie and ice-cream. Meals and drinks can be consumed in a number of cosy rooms and the landlord allows the main bar area, which has a stone-flagged floor to be utilised by walkers wearing muddy boots. Outside, the inn has a beer garden together with a play area for children.

Telephone: 01244 336096.

How to get there: From Chester take the A41 towards Whitchurch. Continue past the Sainsbury's roundabout and after a further 1 ½ miles take the first left after the petrol station signed to Waverton. Proceed to crossroads and turn left. After crossing the canal bridge turn left into Brown Heath Road. At the first crossroads turn right into Plough Lane to arrive at the Plough Inn on the left.

Parking: There is a car park at the side of the Plough Inn and a small car park close by Waverton Bridge near the canal.

Length of the walk: 4½ miles. Map: OS Landranger 117 Chester (GR 454652).

Through an area of countryside only a couple of miles from Chester, this walk takes you from the Plough Inn at Brown Heath to the village of Christleton and back. The route passes close to the Civil War battle site of Rowton Moor, where in 1645 Royalist troops were defeated by Cromwell's forces. The towpath of the Llangollen branch of the Shropshire Union Canal has been utilised on both the outward and return legs of the journey – thus presenting an opportunity to observe at first hand the workings of this appealing waterway.

The Walk

On leaving the inn, turn right to arrive at a crossroads. Turn left here to enter Brown Heath Road and walk along the roadside pavement. A straight 500 metres takes you to a footpath on the right which commences at the side of Oaklands, where a footpath sign points towards Rowton Bridge. A straight 80 metres leads to a kissing-gate at the left-hand side of a facing gate. On passing through the kissing-gate follow the right-hand edge of a field. Pass through a gap at the side of a gate and continue along the right-hand edge of the next field. Go over a stile at the field corner then follow a path through trees shortly to emerge on to the towpath of the Shropshire Union Canal. Turn right and walk along the canal towpath. Go over a couple of stiles and then turn right on meeting a facing hedgerow. Follow a field edge, keeping the hedgerow on your immediate left, then go over a stile to continue along a fenced-in path. Emerge on to a lane by a dwelling called Lane End. Keep forward now, along the facing lane. Pass a number of appealing dwellings and then turn right on meeting a T-junction. Pass Sandrock Road and Badgers Close, and keep on past Plough Lane. Continue past Christleton County High School and a road which goes off to the left called Woodfields. Shortly after passing the Ring O'Bells inn arrive at the green in the centre of the village of Christleton.

Straight ahead is St James's church. A church has stood on this site

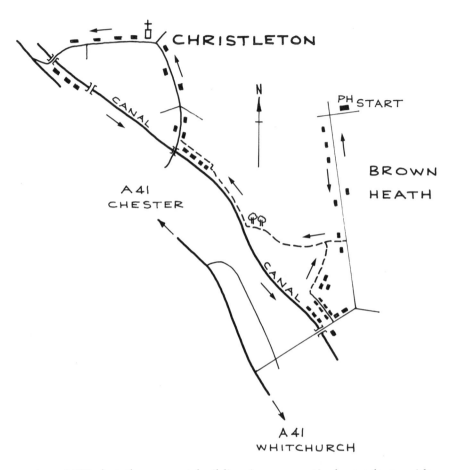

CHRISTLETON

N

PH START

BROWN
HEATH

A41
CHESTER

CANAL

CANAL

A41
WHITCHURCH

since 1093, but the present building is comparatively modern, with the exception of the tower which dates from the 15th century. The church looks out across the village green, where an old water pump stands close to its adjacent pumphouse. On a peaceful summer day it is hard to imagine the havoc caused by the battle of Rowton Moor, when the majority of the village houses were burnt down by the Royalists.

Turn left in front of the church lych gate and follow the laneside pavement past Christleton House, Christleton Cottage and the unadopted Windmill Lane. Shortly after passing Faulkners Lane and the College of Law, arrive at a bridge which takes you over the canal. Immediately on crossing the bridge turn right, to leave the laneside, over a sandstone stile. Descend steps and arrive on the canal towpath.

Turn right and follow the towpath to pass under the bridge which you have just walked over. The towpath passes close to the Old Trooper Inn which takes its name from the troopers of the Civil War. When the canal was used for transporting cargo, narrowboats used to stop here overnight, their horses being stabled at the inn.

A little further on is the refurbished building of an old mill recently converted into dwellings. Pass under a bridge and continue along the towpath. The dwellings on the opposite side of the canal have attractive gardens coming down to the water's edge. Pass under the next bridge and continue along the towpath. It is about 1 mile to the next bridge and in 1645 this was the scene, in the fields on the right, of the bloody Battle of Rowton Moor.

On approaching the next bridge you will see a row of canalside properties on the opposite side of the water, all of which have balconies and mooring facilities. Leave the towpath to the right just before the bridge (No 119). At the crossing road turn left to walk over the bridge. After 80 metres turn left to enter Fox Lane. At the end of this lane, and opposite The Anchorage, enter a footpath which takes you along the edge of a property development. A hedged-in path then leads to a facing gate. Pass through a gap at the side of this gate and turn right, where a straight 80 metres takes you to Brown Heath Road.

You are now back on part of the initial route. Turn left and retrace your steps back to the Plough Inn.

20 Dodleston
The Red Lion Inn

Although Dodleston is only just over 1 mile from the busy A55 along which thousands of summer sun-seekers travel to the coastal resorts of North Wales, it is doubtful if any of these drivers and their passengers are ever aware of this peaceful village where dairy farming is the mainstay of the local community.

The Red Lion Inn dates back over 350 years to a time before the commencement of the English Civil War. Records show that an inn existed at Dodleston in 1640 when the Chester to Wrexham road passed through the village. Although this highway has lost its dominance to the nearby A483, the inn we see today provides an excellent range of refreshments for the traveller. The Red Lion contains an abundance of brasswork and has a cosy atmosphere; do not be surprised if you hear some of the customers speaking in Welsh, for the inn is less than a mile from the border.

The beers are brewed in Cheshire by Bass and the inn offers a wide choice of tasty food served every lunchtime. Food is also available each evening, except on Sundays. The menus are regularly changed and the inn provides a range of meals especially for children, all at very reasonable prices. At the rear, close to the car park there is a beer

garden with trestle tables and benches; also a garden area with amusements for children. The landlord does not permit dogs inside the inn.
Telephone: 01244 660248.

How to get there: The village of Dodleston is 4 miles to the south-west of Chester at the centre of a triangle formed by the Welsh border and the A55 and A483. The Red Lion Inn is in the middle of the village.

Parking: There is a large car park at the rear of the inn, alternatively parking is available at the car park close to the village church.

Length of the walk: 3½ miles. Map: OS Landranger 117 Chester (GR 361611).

The entire walk is along level terrain – although during the initial stages, when crossing fields, there are views to the Welsh foothills. The walk does in fact take you across the border, but you only stroll for 1 mile in Wales prior to reaching the village of Lower Kinnerton, after which a series of field paths lead back to Dodleston and the Red Lion Inn.

The Walk
On leaving the inn, turn right and follow the roadside footpath. Turn right shortly in the direction of Pulford and Wrexham, although you may wish to keep straight ahead here to make a short visit to the village church. Dedicated to St Mary, the church is sited close to the site of Dodleston Castle. On the exterior of the north wall of the church tower are marks said to have been caused by the firing of muskets during the Civil War (1642–49).

Follow the roadside footpath in the direction of Pulford and Wrexham. Pass the village hall (1896) to where, shortly after passing St Mary's Rectory, the road bends to the left. Leave the road here to the right and pass over a stile at the side of a field gate. Follow a field edge, keeping a fence on your immediate right, go over a plank-bridge and stile. Continue, with a hawthorn hedge on the right, and then pass over another stile at the side of a field gate. Turn left now and after 10 metres climb over a stile at the side of a gate and proceed along a track, keeping a hedge on the immediate left. Cross a stile, there is a fence and ditch on your left now. At the field corner go through a gate and almost immediately pass over a stile at the side of another gate to enter a large field. Walk forward to a stile which comes into view as you near the field corner. There is a large water-filled dyke to traverse once you have crossed the stile; take care here for there is only a narrow plank across the ditch and no hand-rails. This dyke forms the

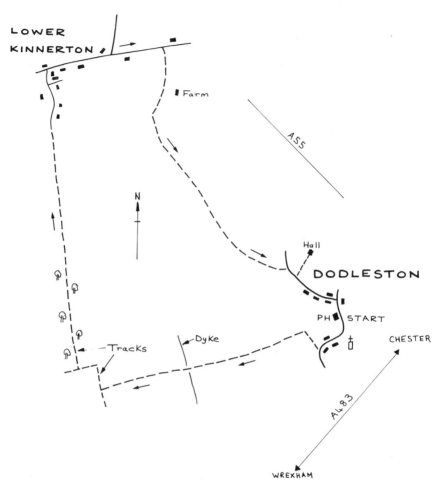

border between England and Wales and for the next mile you will be walking in the county of Clwyd. On crossing the dyke keep in the same direction as before to follow a field edge where there is a fence and dyke on your immediate right. Straight ahead, the Welsh hills can be seen, with Hope Mountain dominant.

A stile at the field corner takes you on to a track where the way is right. Follow this as it shortly turns to the left. After a further 50 metres there is a junction of tracks. Turn right here to walk along a track which is hedged-in by trees on both sides. After ½ mile the track becomes a lane close by low-lying farm outbuildings. Keep forward along the lane and pass Moor Crescent to arrive at a T-junction in the village of Lower Kinnerton.

The way is right here to follow the roadside footpath. Pass a lane which goes to Bretton and Broughton. The roadside footpath finishes shortly, but continue past Warren Wood then, about 150 metres further on, go over a stile on the right at the side of a gate, just before a dwelling on the left is reached. A rough track follows a field edge close to a hedge on the left. Pass through a gap in a hedgerow at the field corner to where, about 50 metres further on your left, there is a crossing place over a dyke immediately followed by a stile which leads you to a large field. Turn right now and walk to a stile some 150 metres away which is about 100 metres to the left of the field corner. Go over the stile, cross a plank-bridge, and follow a path across the head of the next field to another stile about 120 metres away at the field corner. Go over the stile, cross a plank-bridge, and follow a path going diagonally left across the next field to where a gate at the field corner gives access to a large field. The path runs diagonally left and your aiming point is between a farmhouse and a couple of large trees about 250 metres away. On crossing the field a stile at the side of a gate gives access to a lane, where the way is right. Pass the entrance drive of Dodleston Hall and enter the village of Dodleston. On passing the post office turn next right to arrive back at the Red Lion Inn.

21 Warmingham
The Bear's Paw Inn

Warmingham is a tiny rural village in the valley of the river Wheelock. Apart from the Bear's Paw Inn, there is a waterside mill and an interesting church all set in a lush green hollow in this beautiful area of Cheshire.

Sitting in a smaller hollow close to the centre of the village, the Bear's Paw Inn looks out across to the village church. Recently modernised and updated to good effect, the inn offers a wide range of food and drink. Heineken, Chester's, Boddingtons and a house brew specially developed for the inn are all available, together with draught Strongbow cider.

The choice of food is really comprehensive and covers virtually everything that one would expect from an establishment where no expense has been spared on its refurbishment. Bar food can be obtained and there is a fine à la carte restaurant menu. Every day a different array of specials is presented and there is a special menu on offer each Sunday lunchtime. Meals can be obtained every day of the week at lunchtime and during the afternoon and evening and there is something to suit every palate. Main courses include all the variations of steak, gammon, chicken, lamb, beef and fish, together with a wide

choice of vegetables. All this is complemented by an equally excellent range of starters and desserts. The inn boasts a beer garden, a garden area for children, a family room and a friendly welcome.
Telephone: 01270 526317.

How to get there: Warmingham is situated midway between Middlewich and Crewe and between the A530 and A533. The Bear's Paw is in the centre of the village, near to the church.

Parking: There is a large car park at the rear of the inn.

Length of the walk: 3 miles. Map: OS Landranger 118 Stoke-on-Trent and Macclesfield (GR 709611).

Most of the walk is via field paths and there is an abundance of stiles. The initial stage of the walk follows the course of the river before gently climbing to more level terrain, where dairy farming is the prominent occupation of the local farmers. The banks of the river Wheelock are then traversed prior to returning to Warmingham across fields.

The Walk
On leaving the inn, turn right, cross a bridge and arrive at the church of St Leonard. A footpath commences over a stile set in a metal fence on the right here, at the left-hand side of a metal gate opposite the church tower. Before crossing this stile, take a look in and around the church.

There was once a Norman church on this site, followed by a black and white Tudor building. The church tower dates from 1715 although the main fabric is more recent. In the churchyard there is a medieval cross dated 1298 whilst close by is the grave of John Kent. Kent lived at Church House which is a short distance along the lane from the church. Known as 'Rebel Kent', he supported Bonnie Prince Charlie in the 1745 rebellion.

Cross over the stile at the side of the metal gate and walk close by the river shortly to cross another stile near willow trees. Enter a large field and continue along the river bank. On meeting a crossing hedge bear left and, keeping the hedge on your right, walk to a stile at the field corner. Cross this then climb to a stile which can be seen about 100 metres away at the top of a facing bank. Looking back from here you have a fine view across to Warmingham. Go over the stile and follow a field edge to cross another stile after 100 metres or so. Keep forward, in the same direction as before, and on meeting a crossing fence go over a stile which is at the right hand side of an animal drinking trough. You have now entered a very large field. Walk

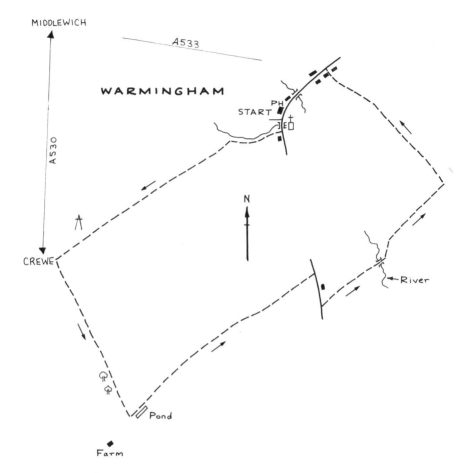

straight across this field keeping about 60 metres to the left of a large electricity pylon. The path takes you to a double stile and plank-bridge crossing a ditch which is protected by fences. Do not cross here but turn left to remain in the large field and continue along the field edge keeping the ditch with its protecting fences on your immediate right.

Pass over a stile at the field corner where there is a crossing fence and continue for a further 100 metres to cross a double stile and plank-bridge. Over this stile, the fence on the right quickly turns to the right, but continue forward here, in the same direction as before, keeping to the left of a row of trees and bushes. There is an old sunken pond on the left here. Where the trees finish keep forward. A farm can be seen now, diagonally over to the right. About 40 metres before arriving at a stile in a crossing fence turn sharp left and with an overgrown pond on your right at first, walk to a stile visible 100 metres away to the right of a field gate. Cross the stile and keep forward along a field edge, keeping a hedge on your immediate left. After 200 metres arrive at the field corner and go over a stile and plank-bridge about 20 metres to the right of the field corner. Continue along a field edge, again with a hedge on your left, then gradually descend to go over a stile and plank-bridge in a thicket at the field corner. Climb forward along a field edge, pass beneath overhead cables, then cross a stile at the side of a field gate to enter a lane. Turn right and walk along the lane.

Pass an isolated dwelling then, after a further 150 metres, leave the lane to the left where a stile gives access to a large field. Follow the field edge, keeping a hedgerow on your immediate right. Join a track near the field corner, then go over a stile at the side of a facing gate. Follow the track and shortly pass over the river Wheelock via a strong flat bridge. Immediately on crossing the river, leave the track and climb diagonally to the left for 80 metres then go over a stile at the side of a field gate. Turn right now and walk along the edge of a large field keeping a hedgerow on your immediate right. At the field corner turn left and, ignoring a stile on the right, proceed to another stile which is some 80 metres away at the side of a field gate. Over the stile follow a path which stays close to a hedgerow on the right and which eventually leads to a track between houses. Cross a couple of stiles here and enter a road where the way is left. Gently descend and arrive at Warmingham Mill, which is on your right. During recent years the mill has been developed into a craft centre. A few more strides and you are back at the Bear's Paw Inn.

Astbury
The Egerton Arms

It is easy to understand why Astbury has become a favourite subject for calendar pictures. There are picturesque dwellings and a village green which is ablaze with colour when the daffodils are in bloom. Furthermore,there is a magnificent church, the origins of which date back to Norman times.

In the shadow of St Mary's church is the Egerton Arms a 300-year-old grade II listed building. As with many Cheshire inns, the building was originally a traditional farmhouse, becoming an inn about 150 years ago. Currently owned by the Robinson Brewery of Stockport, the inn is quite large and has a number of comfortable rooms. Robinson's Best Bitter and Old Tom ales are available, both from the wood, together with draught Strongbow cider.

A wide selection of good-value food is served both at lunchtime and in the evening. Apart from the standard menu there is always a specials board in operation. Food is served in the bar areas and also, if desired, in a separate restaurant. The inn has a family room and a beer garden. Children have their own garden play area. The bed and breakfast accommodation provided by the inn is of a high standard.

Telephone: 01260 273946.

How to get there: Astbury lies just off the A34 1½ miles to the south-west of Congleton. The Egerton Arms is at the centre of the village close by the church.

Parking: The inn has a large car park which is accessible from the village and also directly from the A34. Alternatively, limited parking is usually available in front of the church steps.

Length of the walk: 3½ miles. Map: OS Landranger 118 Stoke-on-Trent and Macclesfield (GR 847617).

Having surveyed what Astbury has to offer, the walk takes you away from the village and out across fields to join the towpath of the Macclesfield Canal. The return leg of the walk is along field paths, tracks and lanes through a very scenic part of the Cheshire countryside.

The Walk

On leaving the inn turn right and then left to pass in front of the church steps. Walk towards the village shop and post office then go through a tall narrow metal gate which is set into the front of a row of facing dwellings about 10 metres to the left of the shop. This gate, which is between No. 2 and Sycamore House, may appear to be a private entrance, but it is a public access. The gate leads to a narrow hedged-in path between gardens at the rear of the dwellings. Keep forward and then turn left on meeting a facing hedgerow. Proceed along a field edge, with the hedgerow on your immediate right. At the field corner go over a stile to enter a field. Walk straight across the field to a stile you will see about 60 metres away in a crossing hedgerow.

From this stile, and almost 3 miles away, on a clear day you should see the well-known folly at Mow Cop which sits atop a hill close to Biddulph. This landmark can now be used as a navigational aid, for the next mile of the walk is generally in the direction of the folly.

Continue, keeping a fence on your left. Shortly there is a stile set in the fence on your left, but ignore this and continue to the field corner. Go over a stile here to enter a large field. Cross this and after about 250 metres go over a stile to continue with a hedgerow on your immediate left. Another stile gives access to a rough undulating, field. Climb forward up a rise in the field then descend and bear right at a facing hedgerow to cross a stream via a plank-bridge. After a further 30 metres, go over a stile at the side of a gate to enter a lane. Turn left along the lane. After 200 metres, arrive at Mill House Farm. Leave the lane to the right here, opposite a small gate which leads into the farm garden, and cross a stile by the side of a tree taking you into a field.

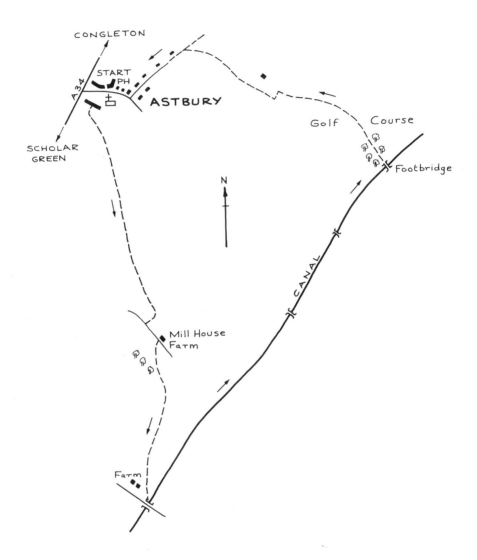

Bear diagonally left, again in the direction of the folly at Mow Cop, to converge gradually with a hedgerow on the right. Farm buildings come into view about 400 metres away straight ahead. Aim about 50 metres to the left of the buildings and walk across a rough field. The going is along level terrain at first followed by a climb up a slope on the left. Arrive on the towpath of the Macclesfield Canal via a stile. Turn left and follow the towpath away from bridge No. 81.

Follow the canal towpath for just over one mile, passing under bridge No. 80 and another, unnumbered bridge to arrive at a foot-bridge. Leave the canal towpath to the left here, and follow a footpath through trees, keeping to the higher ground. Emerge from the trees at a golf course. Walk straight across this, after first checking that you will not interfere with a golf match, then descend steps and go over a footbridge, then climb a facing grassy bank where a small vertical sign points straight ahead. On reaching level ground walk forward and, after 50 metres, go over two stiles in quick succession. Continue along a field edge, keeping a hedgerow on your immediate right. Straight ahead, the tip of the spire of Astbury church comes into view. On reaching the field corner ignore a stile on the right and turn left, then right, to follow the field edge in the general direction of Astbury church. There is a splendid bungalow across the field on the right now. Cross a stile at the field corner then walk forward to another stile which is about 150 metres away at the side of a field gate. On crossing this stile turn left to follow a track which takes you to a facing lane. Keep forward now along the laneside pavement. On passing the village school you will come to a junction. Turn right to shortly arrive back at the Egerton Arms.

23 Smallwood
The Blue Bell Inn

For the past 200 years Smallwood has provided the Potteries with much of its fresh vegetables. Records show that a number of local farmers had contracts with the great Burslem Co-op and kept numerous horses for pulling their fruit vans about.

The Blue Bell is a most attractive little inn, located in a picturesque setting. As with many Cheshire inns the Blue Bell was originally a farm and its origins go back over 300 years. Up until 1939 part of the building was still in use as a farm. With the outbreak of war the farming activities ceased and during 1947 the original building was extended into that which we see today.

Outside a real blue bell is incorporated into the pub sign, whilst inside there is a wealth of low beams, stone floors and antique high-backed benches forming a small enclosure in the bar.

The inn serves a range of Greenall Whitley beers each day at lunchtime and in the evenings (except Monday lunchtime when the inn is closed). Food is served on the same days between 12 noon and 2 pm. The inn is well known for its ploughman's lunches, with generous portions of Cheshire, Cheddar and Stilton cheeses. Tasty pork pies and a full range of traditional and toasted sandwiches are

also available. When the weather is fine, visitors can take their refreshment in an adjacent beer garden.
Telephone: 01477 500262.

How to get there: The scattered rural hamlet of Smallwood lies between the A34 and A50 equidistant from Sandbach and Congleton. From the A34 and about 2 miles to the south of Congleton, is Childs Lane. A road sign here points towards Brownlow and Smallwood. The Blue Bell is just over one mile along this lane on the right. From the A50 at Fourlanes End a lane goes off towards Smallwood and Congleton. The inn is about 1½ miles along this lane on the left.

Parking: The inn has a car park. Alternatively, there is a parking lay-by at the side of a lane close to Alcumlow Hall Farm just off the A34 about ¾ mile to the north of the entrance to Little Moreton Hall.

Length of the walk: 3½ miles. Map: OS Landranger 118 Stoke-on-Trent and Macclesfield (GR 821607).

A walk through an area of the countryside where agricultural produce is very much to the fore. The route is along narrow country lanes, across fields and along tracks where you can observe at first hand an almost forgotten way of life in a very scenic area of rural Cheshire.

The Walk
On leaving the inn turn right to follow a narrow hedged-in lane. Pass Spen Moss Cottage and 20 metres after the entrance drive of Spen Moss Farm fork right to proceed along a grassy track. Just before the track turns sharply to the right at a facing gate go over a stile on the right to enter a large field. With the stile at your back walk forward and pass close to an isolated tree. Pass to the right of a holly bush and another isolated tree to go over a stile in a facing fence. Follow a field edge now keeping a hedgerow and trees on your immediate left. After 200 metres there is a pond among the trees on your left. The field edge turns to the left now but keep forward, bearing slightly right, and pass to the right of an isolated telegraph pole in the middle of the field. Cross a stile and gradually climb to converge with a hedgerow on the right. Go over a stile at the field corner, there is a farm about 30 metres to the left of this stile. Turn left and then right to follow the garden hedge of the farm. Pass over another stile to enter a lane. Turn left and follow the lane past the Methodist chapel which has recently been converted into a dwelling. A little further on arrive at Lesser Reeves Farm on the left. Leave the lane to the right now to follow a path along

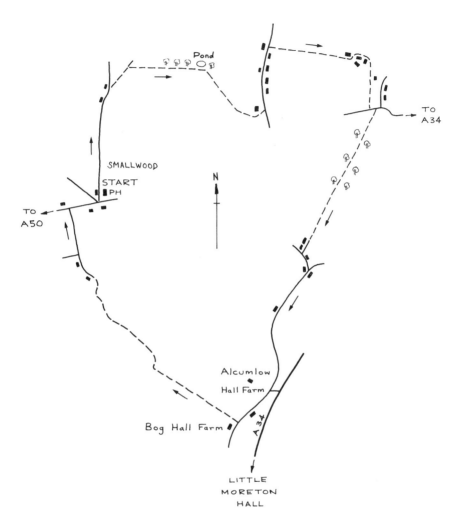

a field edge with a hedgerow on your immediate left. On the skyline over to the right can be seen the folly at Mow Cop.

Go through a gap at the field corner and continue along the edge of the next field, with a hedgerow now on your immediate right. Enter a short length of hedged-in grassy track at the field corner and then bear left at a facing pond. Pass a barn on your right. The way leads towards a farmyard, but turn left between outbuildings just before the farmyard is reached. Bear right now to follow a track between a large low-lying building on the left and other farm buildings on the right.

The track turns to the right by another barn. You are now at a junction of ways. Ignore a grassy track which goes off to the left and keep forward along a rough macadam lane to pass the main entrance drive to the farm on your right. Pass an old dwelling and keep forward along the lane. The way forks shortly where there is a green area on the left. Keep to the right and after 50 metres arrive at a crossing lane. Go straight across the lane and enter a straight grassy track hedged in by ferns, brambles and trees. The track becomes a path which eventually emerges close to houses at Brownlow Heath. Turn next left at the crossing lane and then turn next right by Ivy Cottages.

Continue along the lane and after ¼ mile pass a pair of cottages (Alcumlow Dried Flowers). After a further 200 metres keep right and follow the lane past the entrance drive of Alcumlow Hall Farm. Continue past Chance Hall Cottage and then turn right just before Bog Hall Farm and leave the lane to enter a straight length of facing track leading through trees. The track becomes a path which emerges into a field through a pair of stone gate pillars. A dwelling can be seen from this point about ¼ mile away across the field. The path turns right and then left to follow the field edge, then winds around the field edge to join a gravel track at the right hand side of the dwelling which you pass close by then follow the hedged-in track away from the dwelling. Pass a farm and continue past a track which goes off to the left. The track has become a macadam lane taking you to a crossing lane. Turn right and after ¼ mile arrive back at the Blue Bell Inn.

Haughton Moss
The Nag's Head

Somewhat off the beaten track, but definitely worth searching out, the Nag's Head could almost be described as the archetypal Cheshire inn. In a lovely rural setting, not far from the historic village of Bunbury, most of the delightful building that we see today dates from the 17th century. The inn is a free house and serves a range of Tetley and Burton Ales together with draught Olde English Cider. Once discovered, visitors come from far and wide to sample the excellent cuisine and it is hard to imagine that the attractively decorated dining-room was once a forge where the village blacksmith carried out his trade. Apart from a regularly changing list of 'Chefs Daily Specials', the standard menu offers a wide choice of meals at sensible prices. Except on Mondays, when the inn is closed, meals are served every lunchtime and also during the evening. Starters comprise a choice of soup, pâté, prawn cocktail and breaded mushrooms with a garlic dip. Main courses include trout, fresh salmon, scampi, plaice, various steaks, home-made steak and kidney pie, chicken, lasagne and chilli. Vegetarian dishes are also included. Various salads, filled jacket potatoes and a choice of sandwiches are provided and there is a range of home-made desserts of the day. Children may eat in the dining-room away from the bar. When the weather is fine, drinks may be taken in an adjacent beer garden, at the side of which there is a play area for children. When the weather is on the chilly side real fires provide a warming glow.

Telephone: 01829 260265.

How to get there: The A49 bypasses Tarporley and heads due south towards Whitchurch. About 4 miles to the south of Tarporley is the hamlet of Spurstow, where there are crossroads. Drive in an easterly direction from the A49 (towards Haughton) and after 2 miles arrive at the tiny village of Haughton Moss. The Nag's Head is about 400 yards further on.

Parking: The Nag's Head has a large car park. Alternatively, at the centre of the village is a junction of lanes, one of which goes to Haughton Hall. To the left of this lane, at a no through road, verge parking is available.

Length of the walk: 5 miles. Map: OS Landranger 117 Chester (GR 580561).

The focal point of this walk is the ancient village of Bunbury, situated in rich farming country close to the Central Cheshire Sandstone Ridge. The village contains many old half-timbered cottages and is dominated by a very beautiful church, the origins of which date back to the 8th century. The walk therefore presents an opportunity to explore this historic village in some detail and combines easy-to-follow field paths, tracks, and quiet country lanes, resulting in a pleasant and varied excursion into this interesting area of Cheshire.

The Walk
From the inn turn right and follow a lane which passes The Coach House. Only 100 metres after leaving the inn go over a stile on the right where a footpath sign points away from the lane. This stile is at the side of a gate and is set close to a telegraph pole. Bear diagonally left and walk across a field, aiming to the right of houses you will see about 250 metres away through trees. On meeting a facing hedgerow go over a stile about 30 metres from the field corner and enter a rough field. Walk to the left-hand field corner and go over a sturdy footbridge. Turn right now to follow a narrow fenced-in path which takes you to a stile. Cross the stile and enter a lane. Turn left and pass the houses used as your earlier aiming point and continue along the lane. Pass a dwelling on the right (1895) and a large farm on the left, to arrive at a junction of ways where there is a small green area straight

ahead with a couple of seats. Turn right here to enter a lane which is headed by a no through road sign (this is the alternative parking area).

Pass a mixture of dwellings. The way becomes narrower and leads past a house called Ferret Oak. A few metres further on, go over a stile at the side of a field gate to enter a long narrow field. Walk forward along the middle of the field and then descend slightly to the right-hand field corner. Go over a stile and footbridge here and then after a further 40 metres, go over a stile at the side of a holly bush. Follow a well-defined path across the next field which is often planted with maize, a crop which can grow to over 2 metres in height. The field is about 400 metres across, at the end of which cross a stile set in a facing hedgerow. Immediately turn right to follow a hedged-in track to a crossing road. Turn left and follow the roadside pavement. The road turns to the right and is then much narrower. A little further on, turn right to enter Wyche Road. You are now walking in the general direction of Bunbury church, straight ahead. There is a pond down on the right shortly. A little further on, go over a stile on the right (opposite a dwelling called Wyndhurst) and enter a field. Keeping the garden hedge of a dwelling on your immediate left, follow the field edge. The dwelling on your left is the Chantry House and dates from 1527. It is of box-framed construction and has recently been restored.

Shortly return to Wyche Road via a stile, and turn right to climb up to the church, passing picturesque cottages en route. Visitors are most welcome at the church, which is dedicated to St Boniface who died in 755. The church contains the alabaster tomb and effigy of Sir Hugh Calveley, who rendered great service to the Black Prince. Sir Hugh instigated the 14th century remodelling of the church and established it as a collegiate church. In 1940, it was severely damaged by a landmine when its roof, windows and half of one side were blown out. Thankfully, the main structure remained intact and all the damaged areas were restored.

On leaving the church, pass in front of the Dysart Arms and turn left to enter College Lane. Pass The National Sunday and Daily School (1830). A little further on, there is a dwelling on the left. Go over a stile on the right of the entrance drive to the dwelling and at the side of a field gate. Turn left and walk along a field edge with a stone wall on your immediate left at first. Keep to the right of a hedge jutting out from the left to descend along a hollow in the field. At the bottom of this short descent go over a stile set in a fence on the right. Bear gradually right now and cross more level terrain to converge with a crossing track. The track peters out but walk close to a stream and pass over a broad wooden bridge which is immediately followed by a stile. This bridge is directly underneath overhead power lines. On crossing the stile turn right and follow a well-defined path which is never very

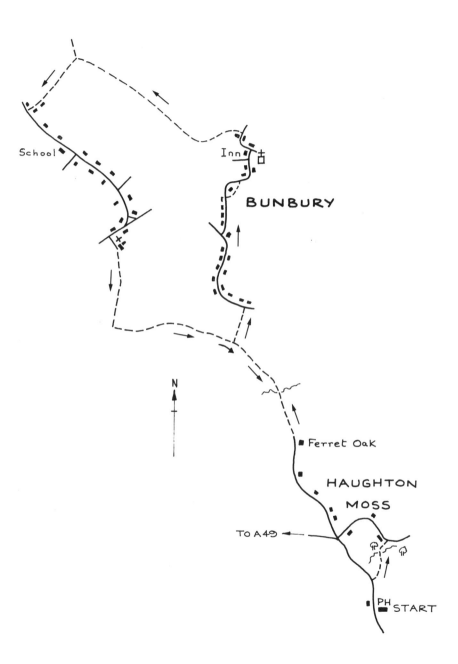

School

Inn

BUNBURY

N

Ferret Oak

HAUGHTON

MOSS

To A49

PH START

far away from a hedgerow on the right. At the end of the field go over a stile in a facing hedgerow and bear slightly left to gradually climb. This section of path cuts across a field corner which is enclosed by evergreen trees over to your right. On reaching the end of the field, and where the trees on the right finish, go over a stile. The main footpath goes to the right but keep left now to walk along a field edge, with a hedgerow on your immediate left. Pass under power lines and descend slightly to go over a stile at the side of a field gate; the bottom support of the stile is a large rectangular stone. Continue, passing to the right of a small outbuilding used to store hay. There is a fence on your right at first now, followed by a large unkempt hedgerow. A little further on, pass through a gate and continue along a track which leads past dwellings and takes you to a crossing road, where the way is left to follow the roadside pavement.

Shortly across the road on your right you will see the well-proportioned building of the primary school. This building was erected in 1874 on the site of a previous building which had stood on this same site since 1594. Since its inception all those years ago the school has been owned by the Haberdashers' Company.

Pass The Highlands and continue past Willow Drive. At the next junction bear right in the direction of Haughton. Pass Holly Bank, an attractive black and white cottage, and keep right to pass a garage. Turn next left to enter Hurst Close and pass the Methodist Church. Keep to the right of a row of bungalows along Hurst Court, and go over a stile on the right which gives access to a large field. Bear slightly left, pass under power cables, and walk towards a stile you will see in a crossing hedgerow about 150 metres away. On crossing the stile walk to the next field corner, about 80 metres away, and go over a fence-stile. Walk along the edge of three further fields, with a hedgerow on your immediate left, and cross three fence-stiles. Over the third, turn left to follow a hedged-in path. Emerge at a facing gate, then keep forward, in the same general direction, and follow a path, via gates, over the ends of three fields. After the third field there is a track going off to the left. Ignore this track and go over a facing stile.

You are now back on part of the initial route. Follow the facing path back to Ferret Oak, and continue to the crossroads at Haughton. Instead of turning left to retrace your steps, a shorter alternative is to walk down the facing lane, where a stroll of 400 metres takes you back to the Nag's Head.

Farndon
The Nag's Head Inn

25

The village of Farndon is, quite literally, a stone's throw from Wales. The majority of its dwellings are perched on a prominence overlooking the river Dee, and a famous medieval bridge links it to its Welsh counterpart, the village of Holt.

The inn, as its name implies, has had a long association with horses. Its situation close to an important crossing place over the river Dee made it a favourite hostelry in the days when horse-drawn coaches were the predominant means of long-distance travel. During the 1820s the landlord, Charles Wright, did not allow women to enter his inn. Thankfully, times have changed and Mr Wright would be surprised to learn that today the inn is managed by Mrs Locker, who ensures that everything runs very smoothly indeed! The open-plan lounge contains a real fire in cooler weather and is adorned with brasswork presenting a welcoming atmosphere. A range of Marston's beers is served including Pedigree real ale. The draught ciders are Strongbow and Woodpecker.

The inn is open every lunchtime and evening for meals and the menu is one of infinite variety, being changed almost daily. The Nag's Head's situation in the midst of an agricultural area ensures that the

produce is always fresh and the inn has quite a reputation for its gammon steaks. There is a board proclaiming special dishes and vegetarians are well catered for.
Telephone: 01829 270261.

How to get there: Farndon, which straddles the A534 next to the river Dee, is 8 miles due south of Chester. The Nag's Head Inn fronts on to the A534 in the centre of the village.

Parking: There is a car park at the rear of the Nag's Head. Alternatively, some limited roadside parking is usually available in the village.

Length of the walk: 3 miles. Map: OS Landranger Chester (GR 412546).

Initially, the walk will take you alongside the river and then along tracks and lanes before returning for a closer look at the interesting village where the walk commenced.

The Walk

On leaving the inn, turn right and descend past River Lane to arrive at the bridge connecting Farndon with Holt. A riverside path commences on the right here, on the Farndon side of the river. There must have been a crossing place at this point on the river from early times, for Farndon lies on a Roman road. Probably a ford or ferry was used initially, followed by the construction of a wooden bridge. It is known that work on the present stone bridge began during 1345 and apart from Chester bridge it is the only surviving medieval bridge in Cheshire. During the Civil War (1642–49) there were many skirmishes at the bridge, for the river Dee was the dividing point between parliamentarian Cheshire and royalist North Wales.

Follow a well-worn path which never strays far from the riverside and go over a number of stiles. There are quite a few weekend dwellings in this area and the path takes you close to many of these. Leaving the weekend retreats behind, the path leads to more open terrain where the fields come down to the water's edge. The river begins to turn to the right; on the opposite bank here can be seen a small footbridge which crosses over a feeder stream. Where the open fields finish go over a stile close to willow trees. A fenced-in path and a rough track take you past an ecological fish farm where a number of man-made pools have been created. The way quickly turns to the left and leads back to the river bank via a stile. Turn right on crossing this stile and, keeping a fence and trees on your immediate right, walk to a gate which you will see some 80 metres away to the right of a

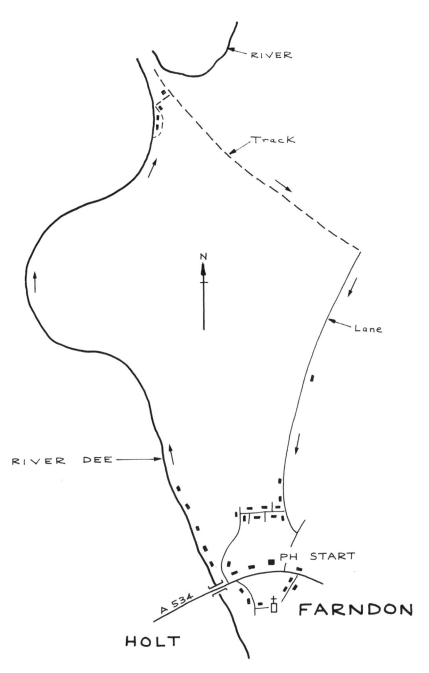

RIVER

Track

N

Lane

RIVER DEE

PH START

A 534

FARNDON

HOLT

dwelling. The gate gives access to a track. Turn right and follow this away from the river. After ½ mile, the track turns sharply to the right and becomes a hedged-in lane. A further ½ mile leads to a small estate of bungalows on your right. Turn right here and enter Townfield Avenue. Pass Dee Crescent and Speeds Way (twice) to arrive at a T-junction. Turn left here to enter River Lane, which takes you back to Farndon close to the Nag's Head Inn.

It would be a pity to conclude the walk at this point without seeing something more of the village; so if time permits enter Church Lane and stroll past picturesque cottages. Turn next left and walk up to the village church, which is dedicated to St Chad. Much of the church was rebuilt following the ravages of the Civil War, at which time an interesting stained-glass window was installed depicting the figures and coats of arms of local families involved in the conflict. Among the memorials in the chapel of the Barnstons there is an inscription to Roger Barnston who led his regiment at the relief of Lucknow on 16th November 1857; he is also honoured by a roadside obelisk standing on the northern side of the village.

Another well-known son of Farndon was John Speed, who mapped the counties of England during the 16th century; Speed was also an accomplished historian.

Leave the church confines along the path leading directly from the porch entrance, then walk along a facing road at the end of which is a rather fine Georgian building. Turn next left to arrive back at the Nag's Head Inn.

Broxton
The Durham Heifer

Once a farmhouse, this attractive roadside inn has built up an enviable reputation for its varied and competitively priced food and drink. The Durham Heifer is owned by Banks's Brewery, a company well known for its fine ales, especially its full-bodied and well-hopped bitter. Apart from a good range of beer, draught Strongbow cider is also available. When it comes to food the inn can stand comparison with any other hostelry for variety and price. All the food is home-made and starters include soup, melon and grape cocktail, mushrooms in garlic and cream sauce, egg mayonnaise and prawn cocktail. Main courses, which are served with chipped or jacket potatoes and vegetables, comprise deep-fried scampi, grilled plaice with tarragon butter, grilled trout with almonds, gammon steak, steak and kidney pie, sirloin and T-bone steaks. Patrons can choose different sauces to complement their steaks including 'The Cheshire' made with blue Cheshire cheese with port and fresh cream. 'Durham Specials' are also available; a wedge of Brie coated in breadcrumbs and deep-fried is served with cranberry sauce. Grilled black pudding with mustard sauce is also on the menu. Salmon, duck and halibut steaks are served and there is a comprehensive and ever-changing 'Specials' blackboard. Sweets include apple and raspberry fool, pear and ginger or jam sponge with custard, and various ice-creams. Hot snacks, sandwiches, stuffed jacket potatoes, ploughman's lunches and other tempting offerings are listed in the menu. Food is served every lunchtime and in the evening. The inn has a beer garden and an adjacent garden area for children. Parties can be catered for by appointment.

Telephone: 01829 782253.

How to get there: Broxton is at the junction of the A41 and A534 some 10 miles to the south-east of Chester. The Durham Heifer inn fronts on to the A534 ½ mile from this junction in the direction of Nantwich.

Parking: The inn has a car park; alternatively, there is a laneside parking area 200 metres along Hill Lane, which leaves the A534 300 metres on the Nantwich side of the inn where a sign indicates that Brown Knowl is ½ mile away.

Length of the walk: 4½ miles. Map: OS Landranger 117 Chester (GR 491543).

Bickerton Hill presents a fine vantage point, offering outstanding views across the Peckforton Hills and Cheshire Plain. Its strategic location was used to advantage by Iron Age man, who built a fortified stronghold close to the cliffs on its north side. The walk skirts around the base of the hill and then gradually climbs across its saddle where the views can be absorbed at leisure. The return leg of the journey takes in the delightful village of Brown Knowl where a mixture of old cottages and farms sit in a hollow amidst the eye-catching hill-country of south-west Cheshire.

The Walk
On leaving the inn turn left, and then left again, to enter a lane where a sign tells you that Duckington is 1½ miles away. After ¼ mile, turn left just before Ivy Farm to enter Ivy Farm Lane. The lane, little more than a gravel track, takes you to a crossing lane. Turn right, keep forward past Broomhill Lane, and gradually climb. Turn next left along Sherrington Lane but after only 50 metres turn right to enter Sandy Lane. On passing the entrance to a dwelling called Tanglewood the lane becomes a gravel track and then forks. Keep left here to remain on level terrain and follow a well-defined track through trees. Shortly, there is a junction of ways. A private track goes off to the right, but keep forward to pass through stumps, where a National Trust sign indicates Bickerton Hill. Go through a facing gate and climb between trees and ferns along a sandy path. After about 100 metres you reach level terrain. Keep forward here then descend along a sandy track where a number of telegraph pole sized supporting logs have

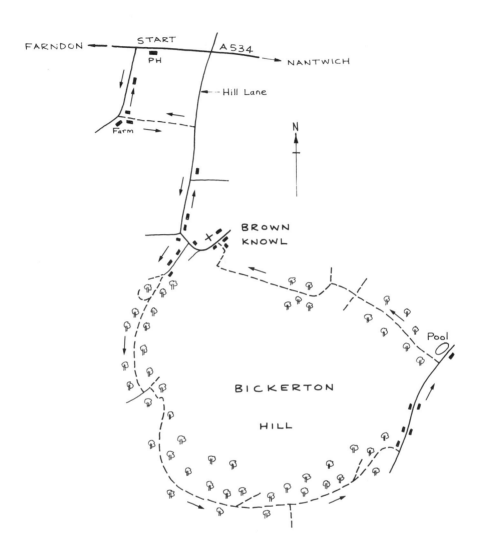

been set across the track about 40 metres apart. Pass through a gate and continue along the sandy track. There are pleasant views through the trees on the right now across the Cheshire Plain.

Pass close to a small parking area and arrive at a crossing macadam lane. Turn left here in the direction of the Sandstone Trail. The lane quickly peters out and there is a junction of ways. Turn right here in the direction of Hampton Green, Willey Moor Lock and Grindley Brook to follow a footpath where the trees form an arch over the path.

111

After about 50 metres, the path kinks to the left up a rough rocky slope and quickly turns to the right. A well-defined track takes you around the base of Bickerton Hill, the bulk of which climbs away to your left. Proceed along the generally level track ignoring any turn-offs which climb up the hill to the left.

After ½ mile, Sandstone Trail turns to the right (over a stile) but keep forward along the main path in the same direction as before. A little further on the path forks. Keep forward here and descend where there is an old stone wall on the right. The path leads through a gully and is walled-in on both sides. Pass through a kissing-gate and arrive at a crossing lane where the way is left. Follow the lane for almost ½ mile and pass some picturesque cottages en route. Turn left just before reaching a laneside pool on the left and follow a sandy track headed by a sign indicating Bickerton Hill and the Sandstone Trail. The track skirts the edge of a National Trust car park, leads through a gate, and then gradually climbs through ferns and trees. Ignore a turn-off to the left and 60 metres further on arrive at a junction of ways. Keep forward here in the direction of Brown Knowl and Fuller Moor but after only a further 50 metres turn left where there is another junction of paths. If the day is clear there are long views from this point.

Descend here, the path runs across open rock in places and leads, after about 100 metres, to a kissing-gate. Go through this and continue to descend along a path taking you through ferns and trees. Emerge from the trees and enter a sloping field where the village of Brown Knowl can be seen straight ahead. Continue to descend, keeping a fence on your immediate right, in the approximate direction of Brown Knowl church. On reaching level ground go over a stile at the side of facing gate and enter a hedged-in track. Follow this as it turns right and then left, pass a dwelling, and emerge on to a lane opposite Brown Knowl Methodist church.

The bulk of the village lies to the right and is well worth a visit although our route is to the left now to gradually climb past Lower Sandy and Sandy Lanes. Turn next right to enter Hill Lane and descend past Broomhill Lane. You are now back on part of your original route. Turn next left into Ivy Farm Lane, turn right again and arrive back at the main road and the Durham Heifer.

27 Tilston
The Fox and Hounds

Although we would consider the village to be somewhat remote, Tilston was an important place when the Domesday Book was compiled.

The Fox and Hounds is an attractive village inn which is steadily building a reputation for its cheery service, fine beers and competitively priced food. The inn is a Marston's house and serves Traditional and Pedigree cask ales. Draught Strongbow cider is also available. Meals are served every evening except Monday and Tuesday. A full menu is available every Sunday lunchtime and a reduced menu is in operation each Saturday lunchtime. Starters include garlic mushrooms, home-made soup, prawn cocktail and pâté. There is a wide choice of main courses including gammon, home-made steak pie, rump steak, roast chicken, lamb chops and fish dishes. Jacket potatoes with a choice of fillings, a selection of salads and ploughman's lunches are also available. There is a daily, ever-changing specials board including an excellent choice of home-made desserts of the day. Children's meals can also be purchased. The inn has a beer garden and a garden play area for children; real fires warm visitors during the winter months.

Telephone: 01829 250255.

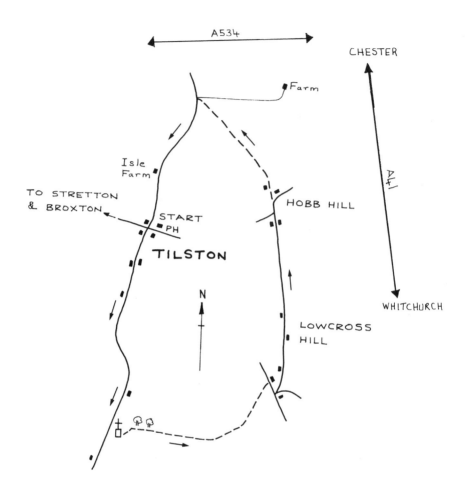

How to get there: Broxton and Malpas are linked by a secondary road running north to south and generally staying parallel with the A41 Chester to Whitchurch road. The village of Tilston, with the Fox and Hounds at its centre, straddles this road 3 miles from Malpas and 2 miles from Broxton.

Parking: There is a car park at the side of the Fox and Hounds. Alternatively, limited roadside parking is available between the village centre and the church.

Length of the walk: 2¾ miles. Map: OS Landranger 117 Chester (GR 459514).

The walk is easy going and takes you away from the village centre along a lane to the rather isolated village church, then out along field paths to the hamlet of Lowcross Hill. A narrow winding, undulating lane leads on to Hobb Hill from where a path takes you over agricultural land to a lane which allows you to complete the return leg of the journey back to Tilston.

It is worth noting that Tilston is only a very short drive from the 17th century Stretton Mill − a visit to which makes an interesting prelude to the walk.

The Walk

From the inn, enter the facing lane in the direction of Shocklach and Worthenbury. On the left are the old village stocks and the aptly named Stocks Cottage. Follow the laneside pavement and continue past the primary school. The pavement finishes here but continue along the lane and pass Tilston playing field (the alternative parking place is just on the left here). The lane bends to left and right and has an adjoining grass verge on which to walk. Arrive at Tilston church which sits on top of a knoll on the left.

The church dates back to the 14th century and has a large stone entrance gate with skulls and crossbones carved into it. The main tower was built during the 16th century and much of the remainder of the building was restored during the 19th century. The windows depict scenes from the Old Testament and the altar rails are dated 1677. The church is well utilised for there is a strong community spirit in the area and many of the old traditions are retained. The custom of rush-bearing still continues as does the annual wakes when a large ox is roasted with the first slice being auctioned and sold to the highest bidder.

Leave the church grounds at the rear, through a small wooden kissing-gate. Turn left and, after 40 metres cross a brook over a small concrete footbridge. Turn right and proceed, keeping a hedge and trees on your immediate left. Shortly, the hedge turns away to the left, but continue forward here to cross a large facing field. Pass to the right of a pond and then walk beneath overhead power lines. Go over a stile set between oak trees. Cross the next field following the route of the overhead power lines. Pass through a field gate and turn left to go immediately through a second gate. Follow a fenced-in track which descends and takes you to a crossing lane via two gates. Turn right and then next left in front of the Well House where a stone footbridge takes you over a stream which tends to flood after heavy rain. Bear left and ascend a lane which climbs through the hamlet of Lowcross Hill. On passing a dwelling called Hill Top the lane descends and is almost roofed in by overhanging trees. The lane dips and climbs and takes you via a sandstone bridge over a tributary of Carden Brook, then climbs again. At the top of the climb pass between dwellings called Hobb Hill Cottage and Finsdale and then turn right where there is a junction of lanes. After 60 metres enter a gravel track at the left-hand side of a dwelling where a footpath finger-post points away from the lane. If the day is clear, there are long views over the hedgerow on the left across to the hills of Wales.

The track gradually descends and takes you close to a rather splendid detached cottage style dwelling. Enter a facing narrow path here which descends and takes you over a footbridge. Immediately on crossing the footbridge go through a gate and then climb forward up a facing grassy embankment to enter a large field. Navigational care is required now. On reaching the more level terrain in the field you will see a farm about 250 metres away over to the right. Keep forward now, bearing slightly left, and walk towards a gate which can be seen set in a hedgerow across the field. Another guide to the right direction is a dwelling on the near horizon which has a chimney pot on each end of its roofline – and this can be used as an aiming point. On passing through the gate turn left along a lane which descends, passes over a bridge, and then climbs past Isle Farm. The lane takes you over another bridge and then gently climbs into the centre of Tilston, back to the Fox and Hounds.

28 Shocklach
The Bull Inn

The village of Shocklach is about 1 mile from the winding course of the river Dee and even less from the border between England and Wales.

The Bull Inn, which was completely refurbished during 1990, has secured an excellent reputation for its food. Home cooking is the order of the day here and the ever-changing menu offers something to suit every taste. Mainstay dishes are items such as steak, chicken, ham, beef and lamb cooked in a variety of ways; these offerings are complemented by a really wide choice of other dishes which change on a daily basis. A particular house favourite is Murphy's Pie, made to a secret recipe but known to contain liberal amounts of Guinness! An impressive range of home-made sweets is prepared daily and a firm favourite here is the 'Bull Inn Sticky Toffee Pudding'. Meals are served every lunchtime (except Monday) and every evening. The inn offers a special three-course menu every Sunday lunchtime. Meals may be taken in the lounge or a large attractive conservatory dining area. The Bull is a free house and offers a wide range of liquid refreshment including draught Bass, draught Burtonwood ales and dry and sweet cider. A range of house wines is also on offer. Children are allowed in the dining area where a friendly welcome greets all visitors.

Telephone: 01829 250239.

How to get there: Farndon and Worthenbury are linked by a secondary road running north to south and generally staying parallel with the course of the river Dee. The village of Shocklach, with the Bull Inn at its centre, straddles this road 4 miles from Farndon and 3 miles from Worthenbury.

Parking: There is a car park at the rear of the Bull Inn.

Length of the walk: 2½ miles. Map: OS Landranger 117 Chester (GR 439492).

Between the village and the river there is a lovely secluded 12th century church which looks out towards the hills of Wales. To maintain a feeling for the sense of its history, this rather isolated site is best approached on foot and towards the end of today's walk this opportunity is presented. The walk is easy going and takes in a mixture of lanes, drives, field paths and tracks through the interesting border country of south-west Cheshire.

The Walk
On leaving the front entrance of the inn turn left and pass the head of a lane to continue along the roadside in the direction of Threapwood. Pass Bullcroft Close, opposite Shocklach Methodist church and after a further 250 metres arrive at Top House Farm. Turn right on passing the farm to enter a narrow hedged-in winding lane which after about ¼ mile takes you past Willow House, on the right. A little further on there is a junction of lanes. The facing lane is headed by a no through road sign but turn right here to shortly pass between Stockton Hall and Salop Cottages. A straight ¼ mile along the lane takes you to a T-junction where the way is left. The lane shortly bears to the right where the right-hand hedge kinks to the right and where there is a metal field gate. Go through this gate to enter a large field. Turn left and continue, keeping a hedgerow on your immediate left. After 100 metres go through a gate on the left, where there are large low-lying farm buildings and turn right to continue in the same direction as before, with the hedgerow now on your immediate right. After 40 metres the hedgerow on the right turns away to the right, but keep forward here to cross a field in the direction of a gate which can be seen 80 metres away straight ahead. Across to the left, in the near distance, are the buildings of Wrexham, whilst on the skyline is the rounded shape of Ruabon Mountain.

On reaching the gate go over a stile on the right and cross a small plank-bridge to enter a field. Turn left and after a further 50 metres arrive at the field corner. Go over a fence-stile and plank-bridge here then continue along the next field edge keeping a hedgerow on your

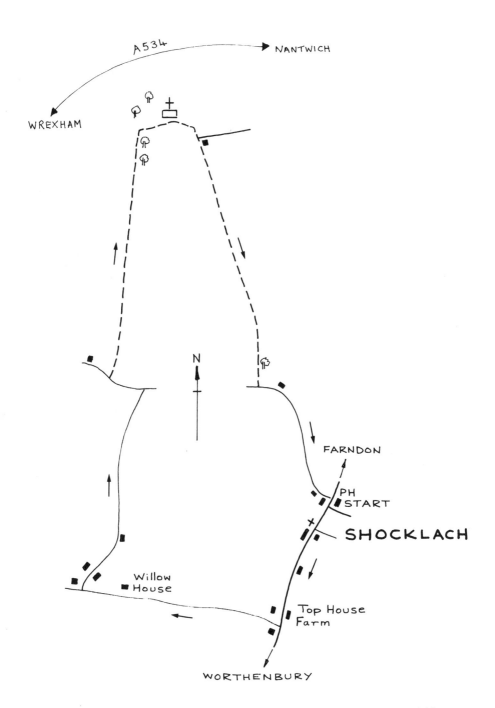

A534

NANTWICH

WREXHAM

N

FARNDON

PH
START

SHOCKLACH

Willow
House

Top House
Farm

WORTHENBURY

immediate left. At the field corner turn right and then left to pass over another stile and plank-bridge. Turn left and then right to continue along the next field edge. Straight ahead, about 300 metres away at the rear of trees, you will see a building which, although not immediately apparent, is in fact a church.

On reaching the field corner go over a fence-stile and continue in the same direction as before with a tall wild hawthorn hedge on the immediate right. At the field corner go over a plank-bridge and stile then walk forward to arrive at the entrance gate of the tiny church of St Edith, Shocklach.

The origins of this simple but sturdy building date back to the 12th century. The church has a pair of exposed bells and over the years the bell ropes have worn grooves into the fabric of the building. Two yew trees used to dominate the approaches to the church but one of these was blown down in a storm a few years ago. A local craftsman fashioned a seat from the fallen tree and this is positioned against the church wall underneath the bells.

On leaving the church, cross the gravel car park and go through a large wooden gate. There is a small isolated brick building here and a facing lane. Turn right and pass between the brick building and a hedgerow, then go over a substantial stile leading into a field. Follow the field edge keeping a hedgerow on your immediate right. After 25 metres the hedgerow on the right kinks away to the right but keep forward here to cross the facing field and then go over a plank-bridge and stile in a crossing fence. Continue in the same direction as before, with a hedgerow on the right at first. Where the hedgerow on the right turns to the right keep forward shortly to go over a double stile and plank-bridge set in a facing hedgerow. Cross the next field in the same direction as before and pass under power cables. About 120 metres further on cross a plank-bridge and stile at the left-hand side of a facing gate. Cross the next field in the same direction as before and then go over a stile in a facing hedgerow. Pass close to three large oak trees and then emerge on to a crossing lane via a stile. Turn left along the lane, which takes you back to the village of Shocklach and the Bull Inn.

Wrenbury
The Dusty Miller

29

The inn enjoys an idyllic location by the waters of the Llangollen branch of the Shropshire Union Canal and was formerly a working mill dating back to the 16th century. At the beginning of the 20th century it ceased operating and became a collection point for locally grown produce which would then be taken to various market outlets via the canal. Between the wars the building was used for storing cheese and in its latter days a storage mill for the then working mill opposite. The building became derelict in 1970 and was converted into licensed premises in 1977. Renovation has continued apace since then and the owners can be proud, for their hard work has created a hostelry of great character and charm.

The inn serves a range of Robinson's and Hartleys beers, and Strongbow cider is on draught. The catering facilities offer a wide range of bar meals at lunchtime and in the evening, as well as providing a bistro style menu. A board of daily specials is shown on an illuminated display. All the meals are home made and vegetables are steamed, three different types usually being offered with each dish. The inn has a charming 38-seater restaurant on the first floor. There is an extensive canal-side beer garden and a garden area for children.

Telephone: 01270 780537.

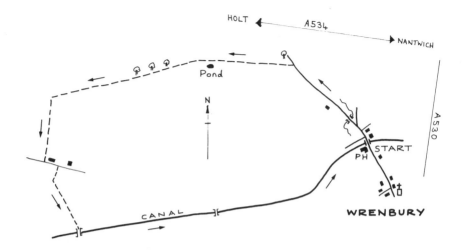

How to get there: Wrenbury is midway between Nantwich and Whitchurch and is situated a couple of miles to the west of the A530. The Dusty Miller lies on the north-east side of the village at the side of the Shropshire Union Canal.

Parking: There is a large car park close by the inn and roadside parking close to where the infant river Weaver flows under a lane 150 metres from the inn.

Length of the walk: 2½ miles. Map: OS Landranger 117 Chester (GR 590480).

A very simple walk – but one full of interest. From Wrenbury, the route initially follows a lane and then takes you along field paths and over stiles. The return leg is along the towpath of the Llangollen branch of the Shropshire Union Canal, an endless source of fascination with its boats and wildlife.

The Walk

From the inn, cross the canal over a counter-balanced road bridge. There is a lane which goes off to the left here in the direction of Bickley and Norbury, but ignore this and walk forward along the facing lane. After 150 metres keep forward, ignoring a turn-off to the right, and follow the lane over the infant river Weaver. Follow the lane for a further 400 metres to arrive at a field gate on the left. This field gate is about 20 metres or so before the first large tree on the left is reached. Go through the gate to enter a large field and walk forward to move very gradually away from the hedgerow on your left. After

150 metres pass under telephone wires and then, 150 metres further on, pass to the right of a low overgrown pond. About 50 metres further on you arrive at the field corner, where a stile set close to hawthorn bushes gives access to the next field. Walk straight ahead now in the same general direction as before to follow the line of intermittently planted trees which once formed part of a field edge. After 200 metres go over a stile near a gate and close by an oblong water tank. Cross the next field, in the same direction as before, and go over another stile set in a crossing fence.

Careful navigation is now required. Walk forward in the direction of a telegraph pole which you will see about 150 metres away in the middle of the field. However, after walking for only about 40 metres, turn left to walk towards the right hand side of a dwelling which is visible about 250 metres away. A stile in a facing hedge to the right of the dwelling gives access to a lane. Turn left and walk along this for about 60 metres then leave the lane to the right where there is a gate. A sign here says 'Canal'. Walk forward and after 40 metres turn left at a facing fence to follow a field edge keeping the fence on your immediate right. The path leads to a bridge which takes you over the canal. Now turn right and go over a fence to gain access to the canal towpath. Walk under the bridge you have just crossed (bridge No 22).

This stretch of canal, which is the Llangollen branch of the Shropshire Union Canal, was opened at the beginning of the 19th century and radically changed the economy of the neighbourhood. Before the canal was opened all the local produce was transported in rough wagons over poorly maintained roads. The canal made trade much easier with Chester, North Wales, the Midlands and Manchester. Today, the canal is no longer used for commercial traffic but carries an ever increasing number of holiday craft and provides enjoyment for anglers, bird-watchers and, of course, walkers! A gentle stroll of almost one mile takes you back to the Dusty Miller.

⓷⓪ Audlem
The Bridge Inn

Audlem is Cheshire's most southerly town. It is a charming place where the parish church sits atop a high mound overlooking scenes little changed in many long years.

Sitting at the side of the Shropshire Union Canal, the Bridge Inn is a charming hostelry which has played its part in the history of the adjoining waterway. The inn used to provide stabling for the horses in the days when the craft using the canal were working boats. Records tell us that Mr Hopkins, a previous landlord, used to ensure that his wife took the horses' collars as surety for stabling fees, for it was not uncommon for the horses' owners to move on without paying. A warm welcome and a friendly atmosphere are guaranteed and travellers can quench their thirsts with a range of Marston's beers, which includes Pedigree real ale. Draught Strongbow cider is also available. An excellent range of food can also be purchased every day at lunchtime and during the early evening. Starters include soup of the day, Japanese-style torpedo prawns and whitebait. Trout, salmon, mackerel and plaice are available. Meat dishes include chicken cooked in various ways, rump and T-bone steaks, mixed grills, gammon and lamb cutlets. There are potted meals like chicken tikka, lasagne and cottage pie. Quick snacks, salads, sandwiches and children's meals are also available. A wide selection of sweets is provided and there is usually a dish of the day. The inn has a beer garden complete with resident goat!

Telephone: 01270 811267.

How to get there: Audlem is 6 miles due south of Nantwich at the junction of the A525 and A529. The Bridge Inn is on the west side of the town by the Shropshire Union Canal.

Parking: The Bridge Inn has a car park. Alternatively, there are usually one or two parking places available in and around the town.

Length of the walk: 5½ miles.Map: OS Landranger 118 Stoke-on-Trent and Macclesfield (GR 659435).

The walk is flat, and easy going, taking in field paths, lanes, tracks and a section of the Shropshire Union Canal – where the boat people can be observed negotiating a series of locks on the approaches to Audlem. If time does not allow, or energy is in short supply, there is an opportunity to halve the distance of the full walk.

The Walk

On leaving the inn, turn left, pass the Methodist church and continue up to the parish church of St James, which sits on a mound overlooking the town. Close by the church entrance steps is a colonnaded structure which is the town's old market hall, sometimes referred to as the Butter Market. It dates from 1733, although its style looks somewhat earlier. Nearby is the Bear Stone with an iron ring to which bears were tethered for baiting. The church, which dates from the 13th century, contains many items of interest. There is a medieval chest and two old fonts, one of which is said to have been carved before the Reformation. The lofty nave roof is over 400 years old and is carved out of solid oak. The stained-glass windows are fine examples. Outside there is an old sundial and a priests' doorway which is now too high for anyone to reach.

After leaving the church, enter Vicarage Lane, which commences opposite the church entrance steps, and gradually descend. The lane turns to the left shortly – where there is a green area on the right. Leave the lane here, cross the green, and go over a facing footbridge. Looking back from here you will see the old grammar school building built during 1655. Cross a fence-stile to enter a large undulating field. Gradually climb along the left-hand edge of the field keeping a hedgerow on your immediate left. Where the hedgerow on the left turns away to the left continue forward in the same general direction

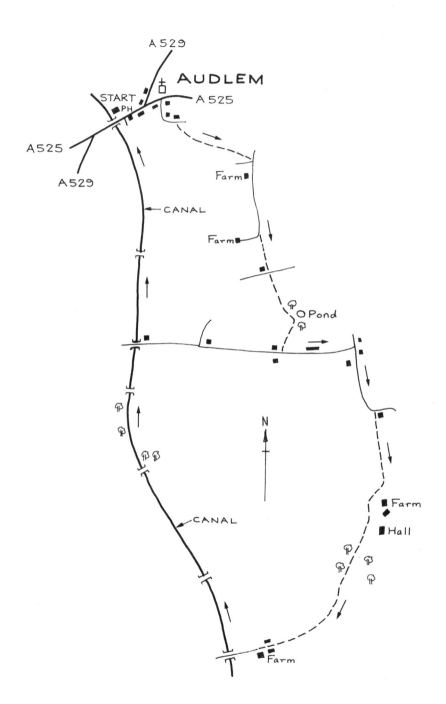

A 529

AUDLEM

START A 525
PH

A 525

A 529

← CANAL

Farm

Farm

Pond

N

← CANAL

Farm

Hall

Farm

to cross the field. Look back here for a splendid view of Audlem, with the church dominating the scene.

Continue to the facing field corner and cross a stile. There is a lane going off sharply to the right here, but ignore this and keep forward along a hedged-in lane taking you in the direction of a farm about 100 metres away. Follow the lane and pass the farm. The hedges finish and the lane goes across open fields, then shortly turns sharply to the right and leads to Fields Farm, but keep straight ahead here to follow a facing gravel and grassy track, which emerges on a lane at the side of a cottage. Walk straight across the lane and go over a facing stile. Follow a field edge, keeping a hedgerow on your right, but after 50 metres keep forward as the hedgerow on your right gradually turns away to the right. Cross an undulating stretch of field to converge gradually with a fence on the left and then cross a stile at the field corner. Follow the left-hand edge of the next field to turn right by an overgrown pond. In a few metres converge with a hedgerow on the left at a point where there are overhead telephone wires. Go over a stile here and then turn right to pass to the left of a dried-up pond where there are rushes. After a further 50 metres go over a stile to the left of a hawthorn tree. Keep forward, there is a fence on the right now, and after a further 50 metres go over another stile to enter a lane.

Note: If you wish to complete the shortened version of the walk turn right along the lane, keep forward past Wood Orchard Lane, and in ½ mile arrive at the towpath of the Shropshire Union Canal via a gate at the side of bridge 76. Walk under the bridge and follow the canal towpath into Audlem.

For the full walk, turn left along the lane. Pass a row of cottages and continue to the junction with Kettle Lane. Turn right here in the direction of Norton-in-Hales. After ¼ mile arrive at a track on the right which goes to Highfields Farm. This track commences at the side of an attractive black and white dwelling. Go over a cattle grid and follow a straight stretch of gravel track in the direction of the farm. About 200 metres before this fork right where a gravel and grassy track takes you across open land. A sign on a white painted rock here indicates 'Country House Salon'. Cross over a cattle grid. After a further 60 metres the track turns to the left and goes towards buildings, but ignore this and keep forward along a grassy track. A few metres further on there is a splendid view over to the left of the half-timbered building of Highfields Hall.

The grassy track peters out shortly but keep forward in the same general direction as before to arrive at a gate in a crossing hedgerow. Go through the gate and continue along a well-defined track. (You have now entered the county of Shropshire in which you will stay for the next 1 ½ miles.) Shortly, the track becomes hedged in and leads towards a large farm. The final 100 metres before the farm is over a concrete surface. Pass between the farm outbuildings and continue past the farmhouse. A hedged-in macadam lane takes you away from the farm and to a bridge which crosses the Shropshire Union Canal. Do not cross here but go through a small gate on the right and descend steps to join the canal towpath. Turn right and follow the towpath away from the bridge. After ¼ mile pass under bridge 73.

The next 2 miles of the walk is along the canal towpath during which you will pass under bridges 74 to 78. This section of the canal has no less than 12 locks which the boat people have to pass through.

On passing under bridge 78 you will see the Bridge Inn on the right. However, before returning to the inn, take a look at Audlem Mill canal shop and workshop which is located a little further on. Great care was taken with this building to ensure that it retained its original appearance. Close by there is an information board which relates the history of this section of the canal and its associated buildings.

A few more metres after the shop and you are back at the Bridge Inn.